MW00340181

Antique Quilts Recreated

CREATED FOR LEISURE ARTS BY HOUSE OF WHITE BIRCHES

Contents

ANTIQUE QUILTS RECREATED ©2003, 2001, 2000, 1999, 1998, 1997 House of White Birches, 306 East Parr Road, Berne, IN 46711, (260) 589-4000. Customer_Service@whitebirches.com. Made in USA.

All rights reserved. This publication is protected under federal copyright laws. Reproduction or distribution of this publication or any other House of White Birches publication, including publications which are out of print, is prohibited unless specifically authorized. This includes, but is not limited to, any form of reproduction or distribution on or through the Internet, including posting, scanning or e-mail transmission.

We have made every effort to ensure that the instructions in this book are complete and accurate. We cannot be responsible for human error, typographical mistakes or variations in individual work.

The designs in this book are protected by copyright; however, you may make the designs for your personal use. This right is surpassed when the designs are made by employees or sold commercially.

ISBN: 1-57486-347-9

Introduction

Lemoyne Star

Whether faded or torn, there is an unexplainable beauty in an antique quilt. It doesn't matter if we have no idea who made the quilt. We sit back in awe at a work of art created by someone many years ago who had little art training and no special schooling but who was able to create a work of art. If you own a collection of family quilts, you are indeed fortunate, for you connect with all of the women who preceded you.

Postage Stamp

If, however, you have to create your own "antique quilts," this book will provide you with the tools to do that. Here is a collection of antique quilts that can be reproduced with today's fabrics and today's quick-piecing techniques.

Today's reproduction fabrics can be used to make your own copy of the antique "Lemoyne Star" on page 27. If the idea of tackling such a large project daunts you, we give you a smaller version on page 32.

A collection of scraps could be your first step in recreating antique quilts. Women of yesterday used scraps from their other projects to create their quilts. They also used other materials such as the wonderful handkerchiefs on page 108. If you have some pretty handkerchiefs, or if you find some at an antique sale, you are on your way.

While our grandmothers were content to piece their quilts with hundreds of pieces, today most of us want faster, quicker methods. The Postage Stamp quilt, for example, on page 115 was originally hand-pieced with more than 4,500 pieces. Here we tell you how to piece this quilt quickly using modern piecing methods.

Antique quilts, like the memory of a child's first steps, have a haunting, unforgettable charm. The mystery, hidden by age, fires our imagination. What gentle hands stitched this fabric and what stories lie hidden in the seams? Create your own "antique quilt" and leave a gift for future generations.

Pinwheel Star

BY SANDRA L. HATCH

Stars and pinwheels have been popular quilt patterns for over 100 years. In this antique quilt, the quilter put a pinwheel inside a star to create this delightful quilt. Since pink and white fabrics are readily available today, this quilt would be an easy one to re-create. If you don't want to try an entire quilt, here are instructions for creating a Pinwheel Star Valance. More accessories, such as accent pillows or pillow shams would be fun to make as well.

Pinwheel Star

Pinwheel Star Quilt
Placement Diagram
70 5/8" x 84 3/4"

Pinwheel Star Quilt

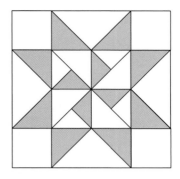

Pinwheel Star
10" x 10" Block

Project Specifications
Quilt Size: 70⅝" x 84¾"

Block Size: 10" x 10"

Number of Blocks: 30

Fabric & Batting
- 1⅜ yards pink solid
- 5⅜ yards white solid
- White solid backing 75" x 89"
- Batting 75" x 89"
- 9⅛ yards self-made or purchased pink binding

Supplies & Tools
- White all-purpose thread
- White quilting thread
- Basic sewing tools and supplies, washable fabric marker, rotary cutter, mat and ruler

Instructions

1. Cut nine strips white solid 3" by fabric width; subcut into 3" square segments for A. You will need 120 A squares.

2. Cut five strips white solid 6¼" by fabric width; subcut strips into 6¼" square segments. Cut each square in half on both diagonals to make B triangles; you will need 120 B triangles.

3. Cut 10 strips pink and five strips white solid 3⅜" by fabric width; subcut into 3⅜" squares. Cut each square in half on one diagonal to make C triangles; you will need 240 pink solid and 120 white solid C triangles.

4. Cut three strips each pink and white solids 3¾" by fabric width; subcut each strip into 3¾" square segments. Cut each segment on both diagonals to make D triangles; you will need 120 each pink and white solid D triangles.

5. To piece one block, sew two pink solid C triangles to B as shown in Figure 1; repeat for four units.

Figure 1
Sew a pink solid
C triangle to B.

6. Sew a pink solid D to a white solid D as shown in Figure 2; repeat for four units. Sew a white solid C to a D unit as shown in Figure 3; repeat for four units.

Figure 2
Sew a pink solid D
to a white solid D.

Figure 3
Sew a white solid
C to a D unit.

7. Join the four C-D units as shown in Figure 4 to complete pinwheel center.

Figure 4
Join the 4 C-D units as
shown to complete
pinwheel center.

Pinwheel Star

8. Sew a B-C unit to opposite sides of the C-D center as shown in Figure 5.

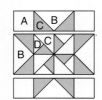

Figure 5
Sew a B-C unit to opposite sides of the C-D center.

9. Sew an A square to each end of the remaining two B-C units. Sew these units to the B-C-D unit as shown in Figure 6 to complete one block; repeat for 30 blocks.

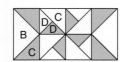

Figure 6
Sew the A-B-C units to the B-C-D unit to complete 1 block.

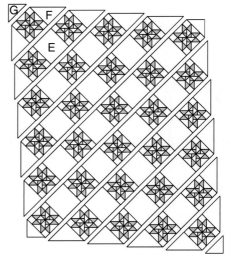

Figure 7
Arrange the pieced blocks in diagonal rows with E squares and F and G triangles.

10. Cut 20 squares white solid 10½" x 10½" for E squares.

11. Cut five squares white solid 15⅜" x 15⅜". Cut each square in half on both diagonals to make F triangles. You will need 18 F triangles.

12. Cut two squares white solid 8" x 8". Cut each square in half on one diagonal to make G triangles. You will need four G triangles.

13. Arrange the pieced blocks in diagonal rows with E squares and F and G triangles as shown in Figure 7; join in diagonal rows. Join the rows to complete the pieced top; press seams away from pieced blocks.

14. Mark a pretty quilting design in the E square and the F and G triangles using washable fabric marker.

15. Sandwich batting between the completed top and prepared backing; pin or baste layers together to hold flat.

16. Quilt as desired by hand or machine. *Note: The quilt shown was hand-quilted using white quilting thread in a wreath design with crosshatch quilting in the center.*

17. When quilting is complete, trim edges even; remove pins or basting. Bind edges with self-made or purchased pink binding to finish.

Pinwheel Star Valance

Project Specifications

Valance Size: 22⅛" x 56½"

Block Size: 10" x 10"

Number of Blocks: 4

Fabric

- 1⅓ yards white solid
- 2 yards pink solid
- White solid lining 24" x 58"

Supplies & Tools

- Pink and white all-purpose thread
- Basic sewing tools and supplies, washable fabric marker, rotary cutter, mat and ruler

Instructions

1. Cut two strips white solid 3" by fabric width; subcut into 3" square segments for A. You will need 16 A squares.

2. Cut one strip white solid 6¼" by fabric width; subcut strip into 6¼" square segments. Cut each square in half on both diagonals to make B triangles; you will need 16 B triangles.

3. Cut two strips pink and one strip white solids 3⅜" by fabric width; subcut into 3⅜" squares. Cut each square in half on one diagonal to make C triangles; you will need 32 pink solid and 16 white solid C triangles.

4. Cut one strip each pink and white solids 3¾" by fabric width; subcut each strip into 3¾" square segments. Cut each segment on both diagonals to make D triangles; you will need 16 each pink and white solid D triangles.

5. Piece four Pinwheel Star blocks referring to steps 5–9 for Pinwheel Star Quilt.

6. Cut two squares white solid 15⅜" x 15⅜"; cut each square in half on both diagonals to make F triangles. You will need six F triangles.

7. Cut two squares white solid 8" x 8"; cut each square in half on one diagonal to make G triangles. You will need four G triangles.

8. Arrange the pieced blocks with the F and G triangles in diagonal rows referring to Figure 8; join in rows.

Pinwheel Star

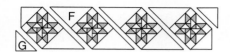

Figure 8
Arrange the pieced blocks with the
F and G triangles in diagonal rows.

Join rows to complete pieced valance section; press seams away from blocks.

9. Cut one strip pink solid 6½" x 57" along length of fabric. Sew to the pieced section with right sides together for valance top.

10. Cut one strip pink solid 2½" x 57" along length of fabric. Sew to the remaining long edge of the pieced section for valance bottom.

11. Place the white solid lining piece right sides together with the pieced top; pin layers together to hold. Trim lining piece even with top.

12. Measure down 2¼" from top edge; mark each end of layered section as shown in Figure 9; measure down 2" more and mark as before.

13. Stitch all around outside edges of pinned section, leaving open between marks on both edges and a 6" opening on the bottom to turn.

14. Turn right side out through bottom opening; press to make all seams flat.

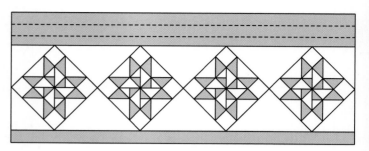

Pinwheel Star Valance
Placement Diagram
22 1/8" x 56 1/2"

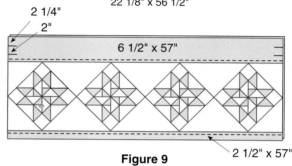

2 1/4"
2"
6 1/2" x 57"
2 1/2" x 57"

Figure 9
Measure down 2 1/4" from top edge; mark
each end of layered section as shown.

15. Hand-stitch 6" opening closed.

16. Stitch in the ditch around blocks and between added borders to secure layers using white all-purpose thread.

17. Mark a line from the 2" openings across valance top; stitch along marked lines using pink all-purpose thread to create the rod opening. Topstitch all around ⅜" from edge using thread to match fabrics, leaving rod openings unstitched to complete the valance. *Note: You will have to change the top thread when stitching the two different fabrics.* ❖

Zigzag Basket

BY SUE HARVEY

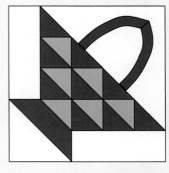

Basket
10" x 10" Block

This beautiful quilt was originally made with scraps of shirting and early 20th century prints, and sashed with an acid green print and a gold solid. Current reproduction fabrics now available would allow today's quilter to make her own version of this quilt. The Zigzag Table Topper, completely made with reproduction fabrics shows how close today's fabrics are to the original. Modern quick-piecing methods are given in the instructions.

Zigzag Basket Ouilt

Project Specifications
Quilt Size: 62¾" x 81"
Block Size: 10" x 10"
Number of Blocks: 24

Fabric & Batting
- 2 yards total dark prints
- 1 yard total shirting prints
- 1½ yards acid green print
- 2½ yards off-white solid
- 1¼ yards gold solid
- Backing 67" x 85"
- Batting 67" x 85"
- 8½ yards self-made or purchased binding

Supplies & Tools
- Neutral color all-purpose thread
- Basic sewing tools and supplies, rotary cutter, mat and ruler

Instructions

1. Cut the following from off-white solid: three strips 8⅞" by fabric width, cut in 8⅞" segments—subcut each segment on one diagonal to make 24 A triangles; two strips 4⅞" by fabric width, cut in 4⅞" segments—cut each segment on one diagonal to make 24 B triangles; and three strips 6½" by fabric width, cut in 2½" segments to make 48 C rectangles.

2. For each block, cut five 2⅞" x 2⅞" squares dark print—cut each square in half on one diagonal to make nine D triangles. Cut one 4⅞" x 4⅞" square dark print—cut each square in half on one diagonal to make one B triangle. Cut one dark print bias strip 1¼" x 12" for handle. Cut three 2⅞" x 2⅞" squares shirting print—cut each square in half on one

Zigzag Basket

diagonal to make five D triangles. Cut one 2½" x 2½" square shirting print for E.

3. To piece one block, turn under both long edges of the handle strip ¼"; press. Place on A triangle with outside edge 3½" from corner of triangle and ½" from edges of triangle, trimming handle length if necessary as shown in Figure 1; pin in place. Topstitch close to edge of inside curve of handle; repeat on outside curve to complete the handle unit.

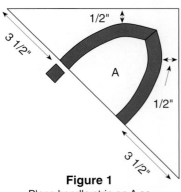

Figure 1
Place handle strip on A as shown; trim if necessary.

4. Place E square on corner of dark print B triangle with right sides together. Stitch on diagonal of E; trim excess and press open as shown in Figure 2. Sew an off-white solid B to the E-B unit.

Figure 2
Place E on corner of B; stitch on diagonal of E. Trim excess and press open.

5. Sew a dark print D to a shirting print D; repeat for five D-D units. Join D-D units with D in rows as shown in Figure 3. Join two rows with D and C as shown in Figure 4. Join one row with C; add the E-B unit again referring to Figure 4.

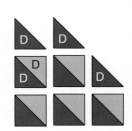

Figure 3
Join D-D units with D in rows.

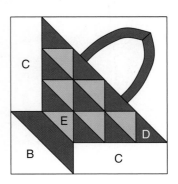

Figure 4
Join 2 rows with D and C.
Join 1 row with C; add E-B.

6. Join units to complete one Basket block as shown in Figure 5; repeat for 24 blocks.

Figure 5
Join units to complete 1 Basket block.

Zigzag Basket

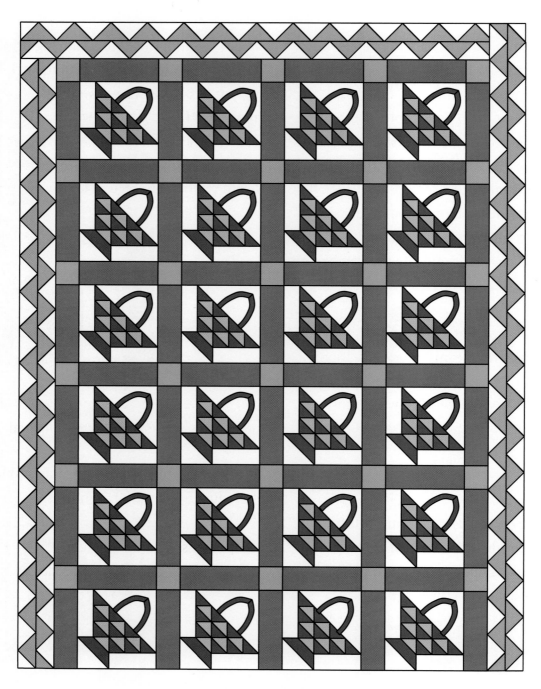

Zigzag Basket Quilt
Placement Diagram
62 3/4" x 81"

7. Cut 54 rectangles 3¼" x 10½" acid green print for sashing strips. Cut 30 squares 3¼" x 3¼" gold solid for sashing squares.

8. Join four sashing strips with five sashing squares as shown in Figure 6; repeat for six sashing rows. Press seams in one direction.

9. Join four blocks with five sashing strips, beginning and ending with a sashing strip as shown in Figure 7; repeat for six block rows. Press seams in one direction.

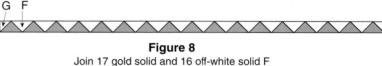

3 1/4" x 10 1/2"

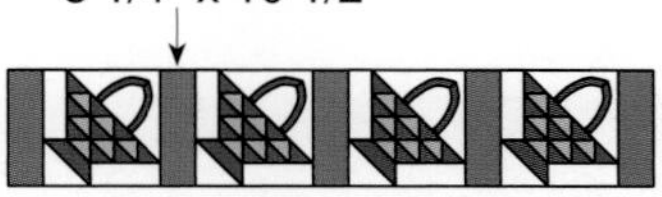

Figure 7
Join 4 blocks with 5 sashing strips to make a block row.

10. Join sashing rows with block rows, beginning with a sashing row to complete the pieced center. Press seams in one direction.

11. Cut four strips each off-white and gold solids 5¾" by fabric width; cut each strip into 5¾" segments—cut each segment on both diagonals to make 93 F triangles each off-white and gold solids.

12. Cut three squares each off-white and gold solids 3⅛" x 3⅛"; cut each square in half on one diagonal to make six G triangles each off-white and gold solids.

13. Join 17 gold solid F triangles with 16 off-white solid F triangles as shown in Figure 8; add an off-white solid G triangle to each end again referring to Figure 8. Join 16 gold solid F triangles with 17 off-white solid F triangles; add a gold solid G triangle to each end. Join the F-G strips along length as shown in Figure 9 to make one Zigzag border strip. Sew to one long side of pieced center referring to the Placement Diagram for positioning.

G F

Figure 8
Join 17 gold solid and 16 off-white solid F triangles; add an off-white solid G to each end.

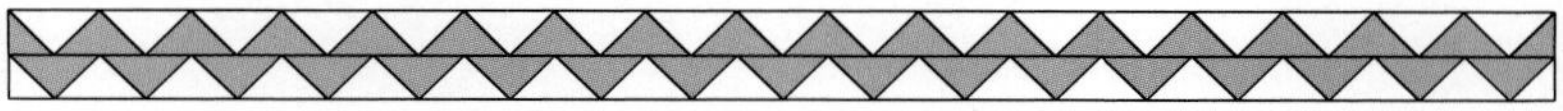

Figure 9
Join F-G strips along length to make a border strip.

14. Complete a second Zigzag border strip referring to step 13 and using 13 gold solid and 12 off-white solid F triangles with two off-white solid G triangles in one strip and 12 gold solid and 13 off-white solid with two gold solid G triangles in the second strip. Join the F-G strips and sew to the top of the pieced center, aligning the border strip end with the edge of the previous border strip and trimming the excess border strip as shown in Figure 10.

Figure 10
Trim excess top border strip as shown.

15. Complete a third Zigzag border strip referring to step 13 and using 18 gold solid and 17 off-white

Zigzag Basket

solid F triangles with two off-white solid G triangles in one strip and 17 gold solid and 18 off-white solid F triangles with two gold solid G triangles in the second strip. Join the F-G strips and sew to the remaining long side of the pieced center to complete the pieced top.

16. Sandwich batting between completed top and prepared backing; pin or baste layers together to hold flat.

17. Quilt as desired by hand or machine. *Note: The quilt shown was hand-quilted on the diagonal through the borders, sashing and block backgrounds. Block handle sections were shadow-quilted in ½" intervals around handle.*

18. When quilting is complete, trim edges even. Bind with self-made or purchased binding to finish.

Zigzag Basket Table Topper

Project Specifications
Topper Size: 31½" x 31½"
Block Size: 10" x 10"
Number of Blocks: 4

Fabric & Batting
- Fat quarter each 4 dark prints
- Fat quarter each 2 shirting prints
- ⅛ yard acid green print
- ⅛ yard gold solid
- 1 yard off-white solid
- Backing 36" x 36"
- Batting 36" x 36"
- 4 yards self-made or purchased binding

Supplies & Tools
- Neutral color all-purpose thread
- Clear nylon monofilament
- Basic sewing tools and supplies, rotary cutter, mat and ruler

Zigzag Basket Table Topper
Placement Diagram
31 1/2" x 31 1/2"

Instructions

1. Cut the following from off-white solid: two squares 8⅞" x 8⅞"—cut in half on one diagonal to make four A triangles; two squares 4⅞" x 4⅞"—cut in half on one diagonal to make four B triangles; and eight 2½" x 6½" C rectangles.

2. Refer to steps 2–6 for Zigzag Basket Quilt to make four Basket blocks.

3. Cut four 3" x 10½" strips acid green print for sashing strips. Cut one 3" x 3" sashing square gold solid.

4. Join two sashing strips with the sashing square to make a sashing row. Join two blocks with one sashing strip; repeat to make two block rows. Join the blocks rows with the sashing row to complete the pieced center, beginning and ending with a block row. Press seams in one direction.

5. Cut 11 squares each off-white and gold solids 5¾" x 5¾"; cut each square in half on both diagonals to make 44 F triangles each off-white and gold solids.

6. Cut four squares each off-white and gold solids 3⅛" x 3⅛"; cut each square in half on one diagonal to make eight G triangles each off-white and gold solids.

7. Refer to step 13 for Zigzag Basket Quilt to make one Zigzag border strip using five gold solid and six off-white solid F triangles with two each off-white and gold solid G triangles for one strip and six gold solid and five off-white solid F triangles for the second strip as shown in Figure 11. Join the F-G strips along length again referring to Figure 11 to complete one border strip. Repeat for four border strips.

Figure 11
Join F and G triangles to make
a border strip as shown.

8. Center and sew a border strip to each side of the pieced center, mitering corners.

9. Complete table topper referring to steps 16–18 for Zigzag Basket Quilt. ❖

Colorado Quilt

BY SUE HARVEY

In Barbara Brackman's *Encyclopedia of Pieced Quilt Patterns*, this quilt is identified as originating in 1941 in the *Kansas City Star*, a newspaper of that period that published quilt patterns. This quilt's maker, however, included a small patch with 1895 embroidered on it that indicates that this pattern was in use much earlier. Whenever it was created, the quilt is beautiful. The instructions here will show you how to use modern reproduction fabrics to re-create the quilt and a runner and pillow set.

Colorado Quilt

Colorado Quilt
Placement Diagram
77 1/2" x 77 1/2"

Colorado Quilt

Project Specifications

Quilt Size: 77½" x 77½"

Block Size: 11" x 11"

Number of Blocks: 25

Fabric & Batting

- 2¼ yards red solid
- 2¼ yards yellow print
- 3½ yards red print
- Backing 82" x 82"
- Batting 82" x 82"
- 9¼ yards self-made or purchased binding

Supplies & Tools

- Red all-purpose thread
- White quilting thread
- Basic sewing tools and supplies, rotary cutter, mat and ruler

Instructions

1. Cut 19 strips each red solid and yellow print 3⅝" by fabric width.

2. Place a red solid strip right sides together with a yellow print strip; cut layered strips into 3⅝" square segments. Repeat with all strips to cut 200 layered squares.

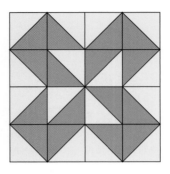

Colorado Quilt
11" x 11" Block

3. Draw a diagonal line on the wrong side of each yellow print square. Stitch ¼" from each side of the diagonal line as shown in Figure 1.

1/4"

Figure 1
Stitch 1/4" from each side
of the diagonal line.

Figure 2
Cut on the diagonal line; press open.

4. Cut on the diagonal line and press open to make 400 triangle/squares referring to Figure 2.

5. To piece one Colorado Quilt block, join two triangle/squares as shown in Figure 3 to make an A unit; repeat for four A units. Join two triangle/squares as shown in Figure 4 to make a B unit; repeat for four B units.

Figure 3
Join 2 triangle/squares
to make an A unit.

Figure 4
Join 2 triangle/squares
to make a B unit.

Colorado Quilt

6. Sew an A unit to a B unit as shown in Figure 5; repeat for four A-B units. Join the A-B units to complete one block referring to the block drawing for positioning of units. Repeat to make 25 blocks.

Figure 5
Sew an A unit to a B unit.

7. Cut six strips red print 11½" by fabric width; cut into sixteen 11½" square segments for setting squares.

8. Cut four 16¾" x 16¾" squares red print; cut each square on both diagonals to make side triangles.

9. Cut two 8⅝" x 8⅝" squares red print; cut each square on one diagonal to make corner triangles.

10. Arrange pieced blocks with setting squares, side and corner triangles in diagonal rows as shown in Figure 6. Join blocks, squares and triangles in diagonal rows; press seams toward setting squares and side and corner triangles. Join rows to complete the pieced top.

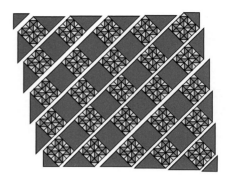

Figure 6
Arrange blocks in diagonal rows
with side and corner triangles.

11. Sandwich batting between the pieced top and prepared backing piece; pin or baste layers together to hold flat.

12. Hand- or machine-quilt as desired. *Note: The antique quilt shown was hand-quilted with three concentric circles in the pieced blocks and a diagonal grid in the setting squares and triangles using white quilting thread.*

13. When quilting is complete, remove pins or basting; trim batting and backing even with quilt top.

14. Bind edges using self-made or purchased binding to finish.

Colorado Runner & Pillow Set

Project Specifications

Runner Size: 21" x 52"

Pillow Size: 25" x 25" (including flange)

Block Size: 11" x 11"

Number of Blocks: 5

Fabric & Batting

- ⅝ yard red solid
- 1 yard yellow print
- 3 yards red print
- Runner backing 25" x 56"
- Pillow lining 18" x 36"
- Runner batting 25" x 56"
- Pillow batting 18" x 36"
- 4½ yards self-made or purchased binding

Supplies & Tools

- Red all-purpose thread
- 2 (18" x 18") pillow forms
- Basting spray

Instructions

1. Cut five strips each red solid and yellow print 3⅝" by fabric width.

2. Complete five Colorado Quilt blocks referring to steps 2–6 for Antique Colorado Quilt. *Note: Set aside 12 triangle/squares for pillow and runner corners.*

3. For runner, cut one 16¾" x 16¾" square red print. Cut on both diagonals to make side triangles. Cut two 8⅝" x 8⅝" squares red print; cut each square in half on one diagonal to make corner triangles.

4. Arrange three blocks with side and corner triangles in diagonal rows as shown in Figure 7. Join blocks and triangles in rows; press seams toward triangles. Join rows to complete the pieced center.

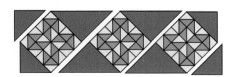

Figure 7
Arrange 3 blocks in diagonal rows
with side and corner triangles.

Colorado Quilt

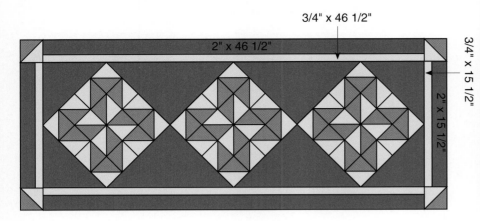

Colorado Quilt Runner
Placement Diagram
21" x 52"

Colorado Quilt Pillow
Placement Diagram
25" x 25"
(including flange)

5. Cut and piece two strips each yellow print 1¼" x 16" and 1¼" x 47". Cut and piece two strips each red print 2½" x 16" and 2½" x 47".

6. Join a yellow print strip with a same-length red print strip along length with right sides together; repeat for four strip sets. Sew the longer strip sets to the longer sides of the pieced center.

7. Sew a triangle/square to each end of the remaining strip sets referring to the Placement Diagram for positioning of the triangle/squares. Sew a strip to opposite ends of the pieced center.

8. Complete runner referring to steps 11–14 for Antique Colorado Quilt, using basting spray to hold batting and backing layers together. *Note: The sample shown was machine-quilted in the same manner as for Antique Colorado Quilt using red all-purpose thread.*

9. For pillows, cut four 8⅝" x 8⅝" squares red print; cut each square on one diagonal for corner triangles. Cut four strips each yellow print 2½" x 16" and 2½" x 20" and eight strips red print 3¼" x 20". Cut two squares each pillow batting and lining 18" x 18".

10. Sew a corner triangle to each side of one block; press seams toward triangles.

11. Sandwich one batting square between one block and one lining square, using basting spray to hold layers together. Quilt as for runner; trim batting and lining even with pieced square. Repeat for the remaining block.

12. Sew a shorter yellow print strip to opposite sides of the pieced square; press seams toward strips. Sew a longer yellow print strip to remaining sides.

13. Sew a red print strip to opposite sides of the pieced square. Sew a triangle/square to each end of the remaining two red print strips referring to the Placement Diagram for positioning. Sew strips to remaining sides of the pieced square to complete one pillow top. Repeat for the second pillow top.

14. Cut four rectangles red print 16" x 25½". Turn under one long edge of each rectangle ¼"; press. Turn under again ½" and topstitch for hem.

15. Place two rectangles together, overlapping hemmed edges 5" as shown in Figure 8. Machine-baste overlapped edge to hold. Topstitch close to seam 3¾" in on each side of the hemmed opening as shown in Figure 9. *Note: This 3¾" is part of the pillow flange. Repeat with remaining rectangles to complete two pillow backings.*

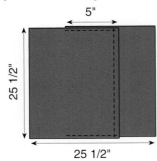

Figure 8
Place 2 rectangles together,
overlapping hemmed edges 5" as shown.

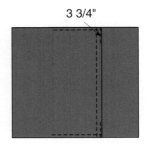

Figure 9
Topstitch close to seam 3 3/4" in on
each side of the hemmed opening.

16. Place a completed pillow top right sides together with a pillow backing; pin. Stitch all around; clip corners and turn right side out through back opening; press edges flat.

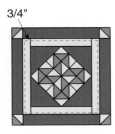

Figure 10
Topstitch 3/4" from seam between
yellow print and red print borders.

17. Topstitch through pillow top and backing pieces ¾" from seam between yellow print and red print borders as shown in Figure 10. Insert pillow form through back opening to complete one pillow. Repeat for second pillow. ❖

Lemoyne Star

BY SUE HARVEY

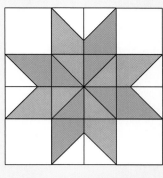

Lemoyne Star
8 1/2" x 8 1/2" Block

This large circa 1880 quilt was purchased at a small antique shop in Maine. The green print and startling gold solid were a popular combination of that era. These colors, however, are easily replicated using fabrics of today. The antique quilt, although hand-quilted, was actually machine-pieced and was undoubtedly cut using templates; the instructions here are for modern quick-cutting template-free techniques. Large quilts of this size were popular in the 19th century; if re-creating the huge antique version of the Lemoyne Quilt seems too large a project, try the modern Wall Quilt.

Lemoyne Star Quilt

Large Quilt

Project Specifications
Quilt Size: 93¼" x 108"
Block Size: 8½" x 8½"
Number of Blocks: 72

Fabric & Batting
- 2¾ yards gold solid
- 4¾ yards white solid
- 6½ yards green print
- Backing 97" x 112"
- Batting 97" x 112"

Supplies & Tools
- All-purpose thread to match fabrics
- Basic sewing tools and supplies, rotary cutter, mat and ruler

Instructions
1. Cut the following from white solid: 38 strips 2¼" by fabric width—subcut into 672 squares 2¼" x 2¼" for A; 23 strips 3" by fabric width—subcut into 310 squares 3" x 3" for D; and two strips 4¾" by fabric width—subcut into 13 squares 4¾" x 4¾" and cut on both diagonals for E triangles.

2. Cut the following from gold solid: 19 strips 3" by

Lemoyne Star

2" x 89 1/4"

2" x 108"

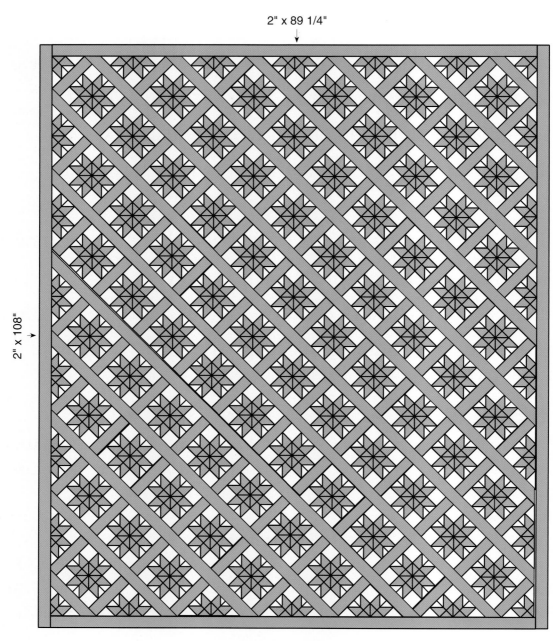

Antique Lemoyne Star
Placement Diagram
93 1/4" x 108"

fabric width—subcut into 336 rectangles 2¼" x 3" for B; 10 strips 2⅝" by fabric width—subcut into 155 squares 2⅝" x 2⅝" and cut on one diagonal for C triangles; and one strip 3¾" by fabric width—subcut into seven squares 3¾" x 3¾" and cut on both diagonals for F triangles.

3. Cut the following from green print: 19 strips 3" by fabric width—subcut into 336 rectangles 2¼" x 3" for B; 10 strips 2⅝" by fabric width—subcut into 155 squares 2⅝" x 2⅝" and cut on one diagonal for C triangles; and one strip 3¾" by fabric width—subcut into seven squares 3¾" x 3¾" and cut on both diagonals for F triangles.

4. Mark a diagonal line on the wrong side of all A squares. Place A right sides together with gold solid B with line positioned as shown in Figure 1. Sew along line; trim seam allowance to ¼" as shown in Figure 2. Open and press flat. Repeat with all gold solid B rectangles.

5. Repeat step 4 using green print B rectangles and positioning line on A as shown in Figure 3.

6. Sew gold solid C to green print C as shown in Figure 4; repeat with all C triangles.

7. Join one green A/B unit with a C/C unit as shown in Figure 5; repeat with all C/C units.

8. Join one gold A/B unit with a D square as shown in Figure 6; repeat with all D squares.

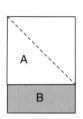

Figure 1
Place A on gold solid B with line positioned as shown.

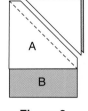

Figure 2
Sew on diagonal line; trim seam allowance to 1/4".

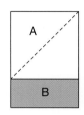

Figure 3
Place A on green print B with line positioned as shown.

Figure 4
Sew gold solid C to green print C.

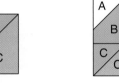

Figure 5
Join green A/B unit with C/C unit.

Figure 6
Join gold A/B unit with D square.

9. Join one A/B-C unit with one A/B-D unit as shown in Figure 7; repeat to make 288 block units.

10. Join four block units as shown in Figure 8 to complete one Lemoyne Star block; repeat for 72 blocks.

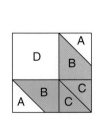

Figure 7
Join A/B-C unit with A/B-D unit to complete 1 block unit.

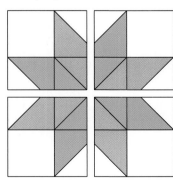

Figure 8
Join 4 block units to complete 1 Lemoyne Star block.

Lemoyne Star

11. Sew an E triangle to a gold solid A/B unit as shown in Figure 9; add a gold print F triangle again referring to Figure 9; repeat for 26 units.

12. Sew an E triangle to a green print A/B unit as shown in Figure 10; add a green print F triangle again referring to Figure 10; repeat for 26 units.

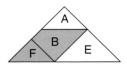

Figure 9
Sew E to gold A/B unit;
add gold print F.

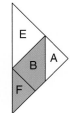

Figure 10
Sew E to green A/B unit;
add green print F.

13. Join one of each unit pieced in steps 11 and 12 to complete one corner unit as shown in Figure 11; repeat for four corner units.

Figure 11
Complete 1 corner
unit as shown.

14. Join one gold A/B-E-F unit with one block unit as shown in Figure 12; repeat for 22 units. Add one green print A/B-E-F unit as shown in Figure 13 to complete one side unit; repeat for 22 side units.

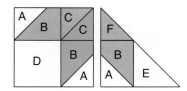

Figure 12
Join 1 gold A/B-E-F unit with
1 block unit as shown.

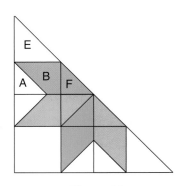

Figure 13
Complete 1 side unit as shown.

15. Cut, and piece as necessary, the following from green print: 84 strips 2½" x 9" for sashing strips; two strips each 2½" x 13", 2½" x 34", 2½" x 55", 2½" x 76", 2½" x 97" and 2½" x 118" for sashing rows; and one strip 2½" x 126½" for sashing row.

Figure 14
Arrange blocks in diagonal rows with side
and corner units and sashing strips.

16. Arrange blocks in diagonal rows with side units and corner units as shown in Figure 14; place a sashing strip between each block, side unit and corner unit again referring to Figure 14. Join sashing strips, blocks, side units and corner units into diagonal rows.

17. Arrange rows with sashing rows as shown in Figure 15. Join rows and sashing rows to complete pieced center. Trim sashing rows even with side and corner units leaving a ¼" seam allowance beyond the intersection of each sashing row and sashing strip seam as shown in Figure 16.

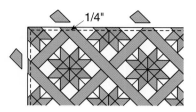

Figure 16
Trim sashing rows even with side and corner units, leaving a 1/4" seam allowance.

18. Cut and piece two strips each 2½" x 89¾" and 2½" x 108½" green print for borders. Sew shorter strips to the top and bottom of the pieced center and the longer strips to opposite sides; press seams toward strips.

19. Sandwich batting between completed top and prepared backing piece; pin or baste layers together to hold.

20. Quilt as desired by hand or machine, stopping ½" from the edge of the completed top. *Note: Antique quilt was hand-quilted ¼" away from all seams using white thread.*

21. When quilting is completed, trim batting ¼" smaller than completed top and backing even with completed top. Turn backing in ¼", encasing edge of batting. Turn edge of completed top in ¼". Topstitch close to edge all around to finish.

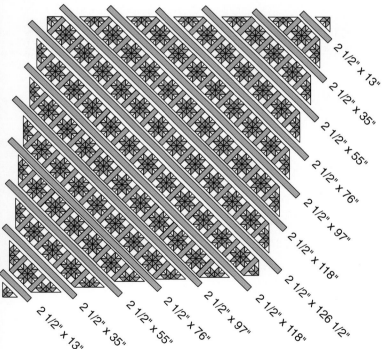

Figure 15
Arrange diagonal rows with sashing rows.

Lemoyne Star Wall Quilt

Project Specifications

Quilt Size: 33¾" x 33¾"

Block Size: 8½" x 8½"

Number of Blocks: 5

Fabric & Batting

- ⅓ yard gold mottled
- ⅔ yard cream tone-on-tone print
- 1 yard green print
- Backing 38" x 38"
- Batting 38" x 38"
- 4 yards self-made or purchased binding

Supplies & Tools

- All-purpose thread to match fabrics
- Clear nylon monofilament
- Basic sewing tools and supplies, rotary cutter, mat and ruler

Instructions

1. Cut the following from cream tone-on-tone print: four strips 2¼" by fabric width—subcut into 64 squares 2¼" x 2¼" for A; two strips 3" by fabric width—subcut into 24 squares 3" x 3" for D; and four 4¾" x 4¾" squares—cut on both diagonals for E triangles.

2. Cut the following from gold mottled: two strips 3" by fabric width—subcut into 32 rectangles 2¼" x 3" for B; one strip 2⅝" by fabric width—subcut into 12 squares 2⅝" x 2⅝" and cut on one diagonal to make C triangles; and two squares 3¾" x 3¾"—cut on both diagonals for F triangles.

3. Cut the following from green print: two strips 3" by fabric width—subcut into 32 rectangles 2¼" x 3" for B; one strip 2⅝" by fabric width—subcut into 12 squares 2⅝" x 2⅝" and cut on one diagonal to make C triangles; and two squares 3¾" x 3¾"—cut on both diagonals for F triangles.

4. Make five Lemoyne Star blocks, four corner units and four side units referring to steps 4–14 for antique Lemoyne Star Quilt.

5. Cut the following from green print: eight 2½" x 9" sashing strips and two strips each 2½" x 13" and 2½" x 34" for sashing rows.

6. Complete the pieced top referring to steps 16–18 of the instructions for antique Lemoyne Star Quilt and to Figure 17 for arrangement of sashing strips and rows.

7. Cut two strips each 2½" x 30¼" and 2½" x 34¼" green print for borders. Sew shorter strips to opposite sides of the pieced center and the longer strips to remaining sides; press seams toward strips.

8. Sandwich batting between completed top and pre-pared backing piece; pin or baste layers together to hold.

9. Quilt as desired by hand or machine. When quilting is complete, trim edges even. *Note: Sample project was machine-quilted ¼" from seams using clear nylon monofilament in the top of the machine and all-purpose thread in the bobbin.*

10. Bind edges with self-made or purchased binding to finish. ❖

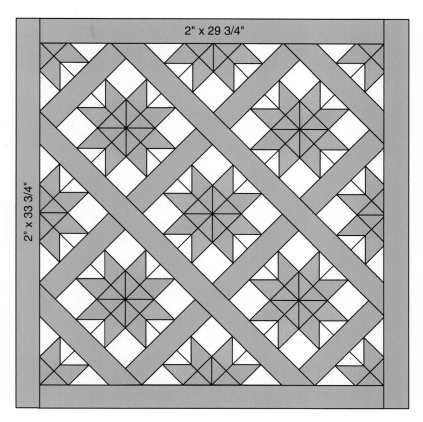

Lemoyne Star Wall Quilt
Placement Diagram
33 3/4" x 33 3/4"

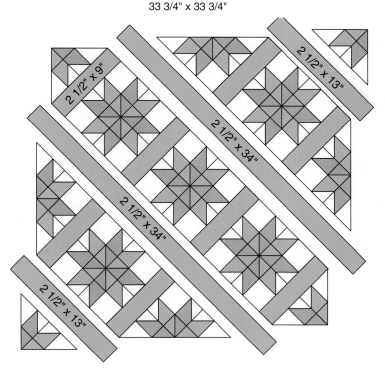

Figure 17
Arrange wall quilt blocks in diagonal rows with side and corner units and sashing strips and rows.

Sunshine Aster

BY CAROL SCHERER

We often will not know who made an antique quilt, but we know that the maker of this quilt loved fine hand quilting. She spent very little energy piecing—there is only one template repeated many times— but she not only left plain blocks to be filled with hand quilting, she included a quilting pattern in the center of her pieced blocks. She finished the quilt with a scalloped edge; we have simplified the process by giving instructions for a straight border. If you love hand quilting— or if you are an expert at machine quilting—this is the quilt for you.

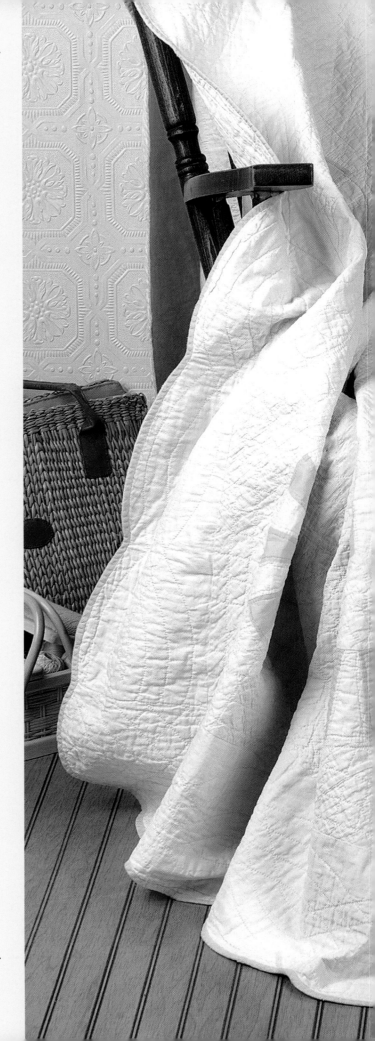

Sunshine Aster

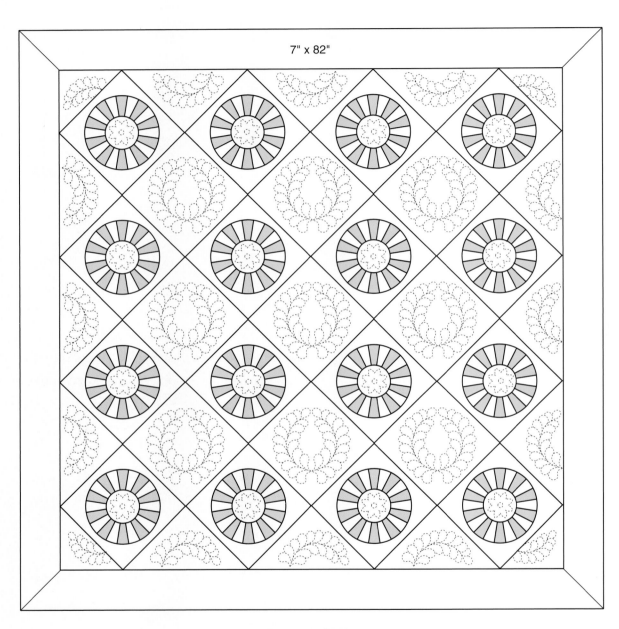

7" x 82"

Sunshine Aster
Placement Diagram
82" x 82"

Sunshine Aster

Project Specifications

Quilt Size: 82" x 82"
Block Size: 12" x 12"

Fabric & Batting

- 1 yard yellow solid
- 7 yards white solid
- Batting 86" x 86"
- Backing 86" x 86"
- 10 yards self-made or purchased binding

Supplies & Tools

- White all-purpose thread
- White hand-quilting thread
- Basic sewing supplies and tools
- Water-erasible marker

Instructions

1. Prepare template for pattern piece A. Cut as directed for one block. Repeat for 16 blocks.

2. To piece one block, sew two yellow A's to three white A's as shown in Figure 1; repeat for two sections. Sew two white A's to three yellow A's, again referring to Figure 1. Join one section of each color combination make half the block; repeat. Join the two halves to complete the piecing; press seams in one direction. Repeat for 16 pieced units.

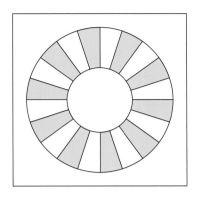

Aster
12" x 12" Block

3. Cut 25 white solid blocks 12½" x 12½". Set aside nine blocks. Fold the remaining 16 blocks in quarters; crease to mark centers.

4. Center a pieced unit on one square using crease lines as guides for placement. Turn edges of pieced unit under both on outside and inside edges; appliqué in place. Repeat for 16 blocks.

5. Cut two white solid squares 9⅜" x 9⅜"; cut in half on the diagonal once to make corner squares as shown in Figure 2.

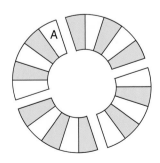

Figure 1
Piece A sections as shown.

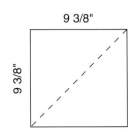

9 3/8"

9 3/8"

Figure 2
Cut 9 3/8" squares once on the diagonal to make corner triangles.

Sunshine Aster

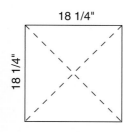

18 1/4"

18 1/4"

Figure 3
Cut 18 1/4" squares on
each diagonal to make
side fill-in triangles.

6. Cut three white solid squares 18¼" x 18¼". Cut each square in half on both diagonals to make side fill-in triangles as shown in Figure 3.

7. Arrange the pieced/appliquéd blocks in diagonal rows with the solid blocks and corner and side fill-in triangles as shown in Figure 4. Join in rows; join rows to complete top; press.

Figure 4
Arrange blocks and triangles in diagonal rows as shown.

8. Cut four border strips white solid 7½" x 82½". Sew a strip to each side, mitering corners; press. *Note: The quilt shown has a scalloped edge. No instructions or patterns are given for this edge finish.*

9. Mark the quilting designs given onto the top using a water-erasable pencil or marker referring to the Placement Diagram and Figure 5 for placement.

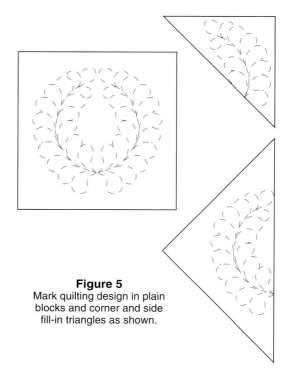

Figure 5
Mark quilting design in plain blocks and corner and side fill-in triangles as shown.

10. Sandwich batting between the completed top and prepared backing piece. Baste layers together to hold flat.

11. Quilt on marked lines and as desired. When quilting is complete, trim edges even.

12. Bind edges with self-made or purchased binding to finish. ❖

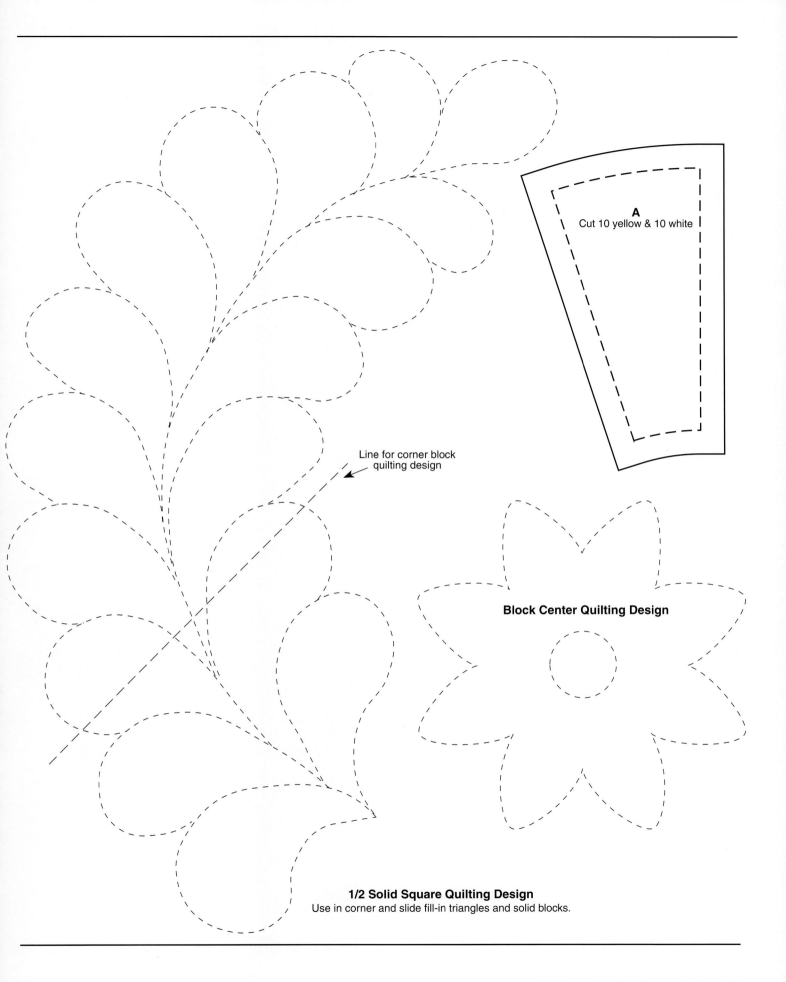

A
Cut 10 yellow & 10 white

Line for corner block
quilting design

Block Center Quilting Design

1/2 Solid Square Quilting Design
Use in corner and slide fill-in triangles and solid blocks.

Kansas Troubles

BY PAULINE LEHMAN

This unquilted quilt top was discovered by the quilt maker's relatives in her attic after her death. No one in the family suspected that dear Aunt Pauline had completed the top and stored it away. Members of the family got together and hand-quilted it so that it could be used. With the reproduction fabrics available today, this beautiful quilt could be re-created with ease.

Kansas Troubles

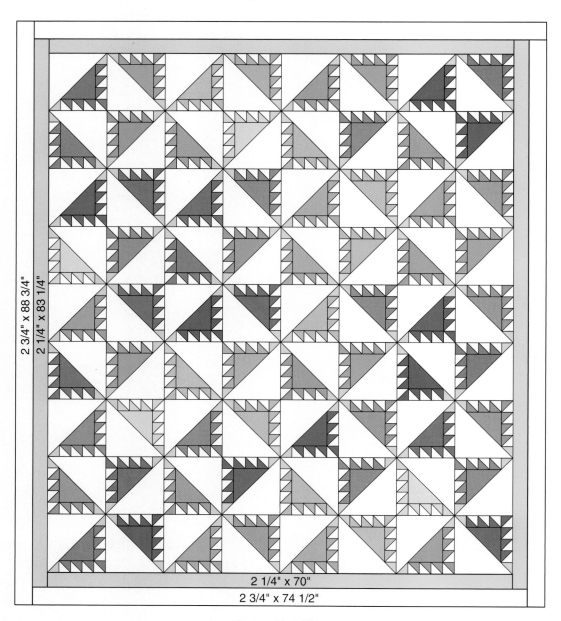

Kansas Troubles
Placement Diagram
80" x 88 3/4"

Kansas Troubles

Project Specifications

Quilt Size: 80" x 88¾"

Block Size: 8¾" x 8¾"

Number of Blocks: 72

Fabric & Batting

- 3 yards yellow solid
- 72 scrap print squares 10" x 10"
- 4 yards white solid
- Backing 84" x 93"
- Batting 84" x 93"
- 9½ yards self-made or purchased binding

Supplies & Tools

- White all-purpose thread
- White hand-quilting thread
- Basic sewing supplies and tools

Instructions

1. Prepare templates using pattern pieces given. Cut as directed on each piece for one block; repeat for 72 blocks.

2. Sew a white A to a print A as shown in Figure 1; repeat for seven A/A units.

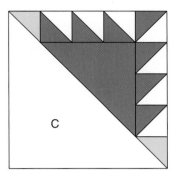

Kansas Troubles Variation
8 3/4" x 8 3/4" Block

3. Join three scrap/white A units as shown in Figure 2. Join four scrap/white A units; add yellow A triangles to one end of each unit again referring to Figure 2.

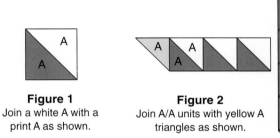

Figure 1
Join a white A with a print A as shown.

Figure 2
Join A/A units with yellow A triangles as shown.

4. Sew the A units to B as shown in Figure 3. Sew this unit to C to complete one block; press. Repeat for 72 blocks.

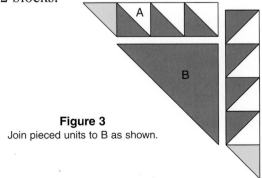

Figure 3
Join pieced units to B as shown.

Kansas Troubles

5. Arrange the blocks in nine rows of eight blocks each, referring to Figure 4 for two row variations. Join the rows, referring to the Placement Diagram for positioning.

Make 5

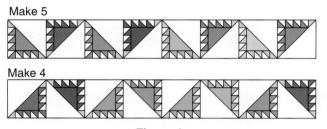

Make 4

Figure 4
Join blocks in rows as shown.

6. Cut two strips yellow print 2¾" x 70½"; sew a strip to top and bottom of pieced center. Press seams toward strips. Cut two more strips yellow print 2¾" x 83¾"; sew a strip to opposite sides of pieced center. Press seams toward strips.

7. Cut two strips white solid 3¼" x 75"; sew a strip to top and bottom of pieced center. Press seams toward strips. Cut two more strips white solid 3¼" x 89¼"; sew a strip to opposite sides of pieced center. Press seams toward strips.

8. Sandwich batting between completed top and prepared backing piece. Pin or baste layers together to hold flat. Quilt as desired using white quilting thread.

9. When quilting is complete, trim edges even. Bind with self-made or purchased binding to finish. ❖

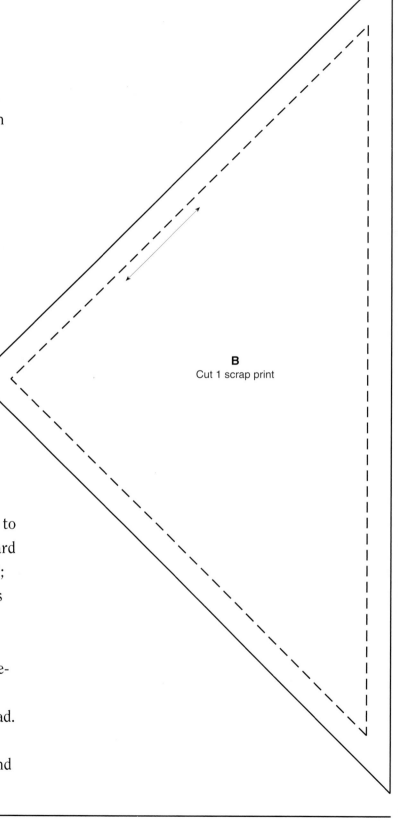

B
Cut 1 scrap print

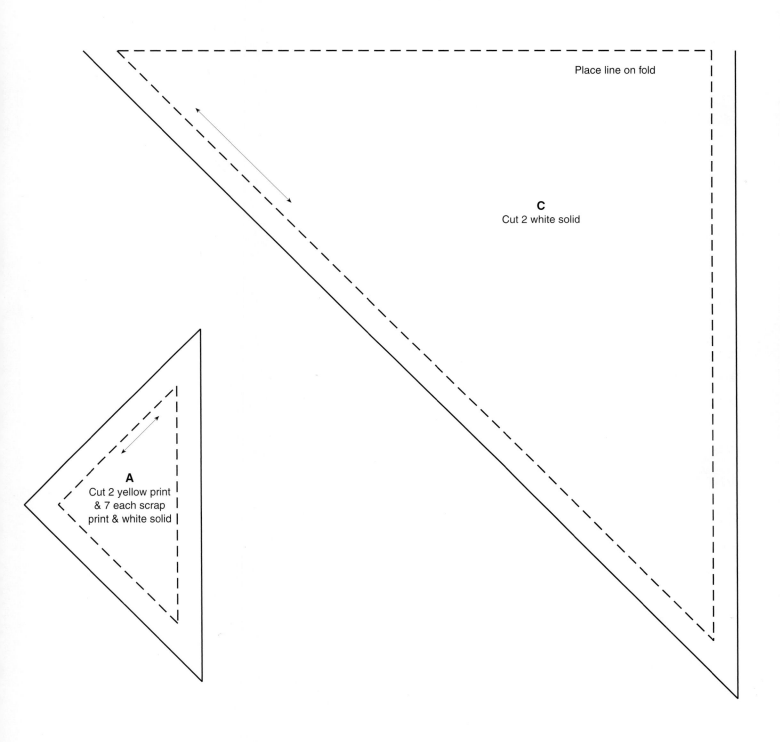

Place line on fold

C
Cut 2 white solid

A
Cut 2 yellow print
& 7 each scrap
print & white solid

Anne's Basket

BY JILL REBER

Adapted from a photo of a 1930s basket quilt, this quilt was created by the members of "The Twisted Sisters," a small quilting group, for their fellow member, Anne, who had expressed a desire for an old-fashioned 30s basket quilt with pastel fabrics for the baskets. There are two sets of instructions: the traditional method, which uses the templates that would have been used to make this quilt in the 1930s and the quicker, no-template method so popular today.

Anne's Basket

Anne's Basket
Placement Diagram
Approximately 94 1/2" x 109"

Anne's Basket

Project Specifications

Quilt Size: Approximately 94½" x 109"

Block Size: 10" x 10"

Number of Blocks: 30

Fabric & Batting

- 30 assorted pastel print strips 8" x 22"
- 4 yards white solid
- 5 yards yellow solid
- Backing 99" x 113"
- Batting 99" x 113"
- 12 yards self-made or purchased binding

Supplies & Tools

- White and neutral color all-purpose thread
- White quilting thread
- Basic sewing supplies and tools

Traditional Method

1. Prepare templates using pattern pieces given. Cut as directed on each piece for one block; repeat for 30 blocks.

2. Sew a white B to a print B; repeat for six units. Sew a white C to a print C. Sew a print B to D; repeat. Arrange pieced units with A and E as shown in Figure 1. Join units to complete one block; repeat for 30 blocks and press.

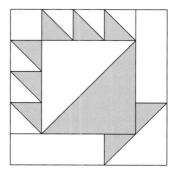

Anne's Basket
10" x 10" Block

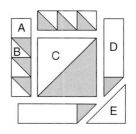

Figure 1
Lay out units as shown.

3. Cut 20 squares yellow solid 10½" x 10½". Cut five squares yellow solid 15⅜" x 15⅜". Cut each square in half on both diagonals for F fill-in triangles. Cut two yellow solid squares 7⅞" x 7⅞". Cut each square in half on one diagonal for G corner triangles.

4. Arrange pieced blocks with yellow squares and F and G triangles in diagonal rows as shown in Figure 2. Join to make rows; join rows to complete pieced center. Press seams in one direction.

5. Cut four strips each white solid and two strips each yellow solid 4½" x 98" and 4½" x 112". Sew a 112" white strip to a 112" yellow strip to a 112" white strip; press seams in one direction. Repeat for second strip set. Sew a 98" white strip to a 98"

Anne's Basket

yellow strip to a 98" white strip; press seam in one direction. Repeat for second strip set.

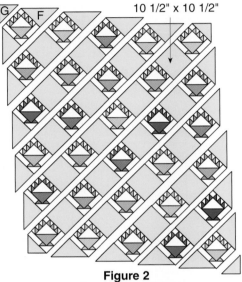

10 1/2" x 10 1/2"

Figure 2
Arrange pieced blocks with solid blocks
and F and G triangles in diagonal rows.

6. Fold each strip set to find center; mark with a pin. Match the centers of each strip to the centers of the quilt sides and top and bottom, pinning longer strips to sides and shorter strips to top and bottom.

7. Stitch strips in place, starting and stopping stitching at seam allowance. Miter corners; trim excess from underneath and press.

8. Mark a chosen quilting design on yellow solid blocks, in C triangles on blocks and on border strips.

9. Sandwich batting between completed top and prepared backing piece. Pin or baste layers together to hold flat. Quilt as desired by hand or machine using white quilting thread.

10. When quilting is complete, trim edges even. Bind with self-made or purchased binding to finish.

Quicker Method

1. Cut the following from white solid: seven strips $2\frac{7}{8}$" by fabric width (cut into 90 segments $2\frac{7}{8}$"); two strips $4\frac{7}{8}$" by fabric width (cut into twelve $4\frac{7}{8}$" segments); three strips $6\frac{7}{8}$" by fabric width (cut into

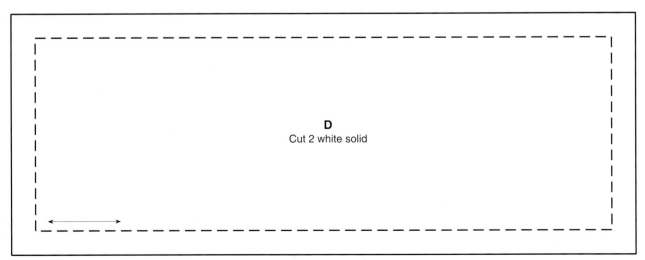

D
Cut 2 white solid

fifteen 6⅞" segments); 60 rectangles 2½" x 6½" for D; and 30 squares 2½" x 2½" for A. Cut the 2⅞" x 2⅞", 4⅞" x 4⅞" and 6⅞" x 6⅞" squares in half on one diagonal to make B, C and E triangles.

2. From each of the print strips cut one square 6⅞" x

6⅞" and four squares 2⅞" x 2⅞". Cut all squares in half on one diagonal to make C and B triangles.

3. Piece blocks and complete quilt as for Traditional Method. ❖

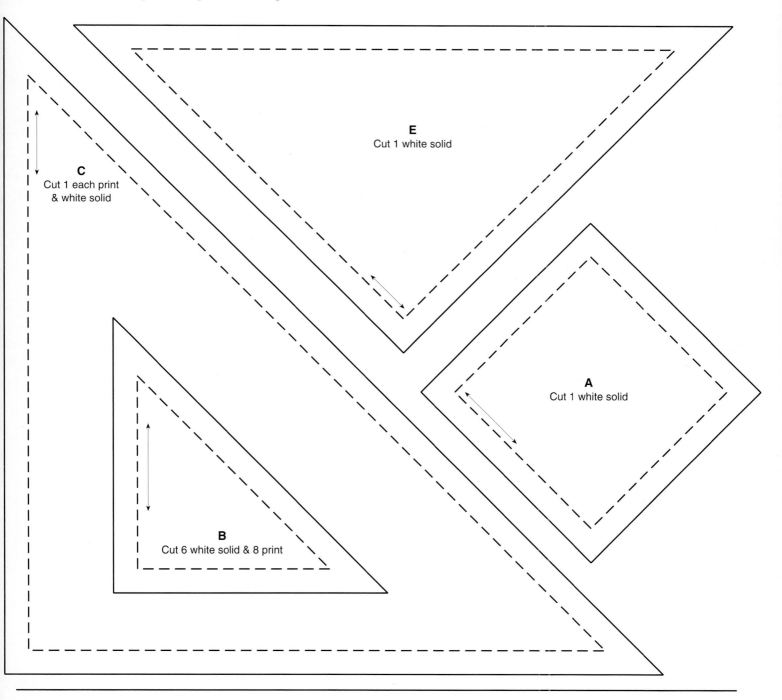

E
Cut 1 white solid

C
Cut 1 each print
& white solid

A
Cut 1 white solid

B
Cut 6 white solid & 8 print

Bow Tie

BY SUE HARVEY

The blocks in this antique quilt were made with assorted light shirt scraps and darker prints, gingham and stripes dating from late 1800s to the early 1900s. Templates were used to cut the pieces for the bow ties, and background pieces were then set into the pieced bow ties. Directions are given here to make the blocks using quick-piecing techniques with no set-in pieces. In the antique quilt, most of the blocks were made with light bow ties and darker backgrounds; however, 11 blocks were made in the opposite combination and inserted randomly into the rows. The cutting instructions here will produce only light bow ties, but if you substitute darker fabrics for some of the ties in some of the blocks, your quilt will be more faithful to the antique version. Before you start the quilt, you may want to make the Bow Tie box on page 57. It makes the perfect companion to your quilt.

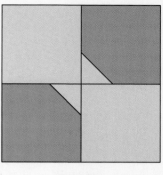

Bow Tie
5" x 5" Block

Bow Tie Quilt

Project Specifications
Quilt Size: 64⅛" x 67⅛"
Block Size: 5" x 5"
Number of Blocks: 81

Fabric & Batting
- 1 yard total dark scraps
- 1½ yards total light scraps
- 2½ yards green print
- Backing 69" x 72"
- Thin batting 69" x 72"
- 7¾ yards self-made or purchased binding

Supplies & Tools
- Neutral color all-purpose thread
- White quilting thread
- Basic sewing tools and supplies, rotary cutter, mat and ruler

Bow Tie

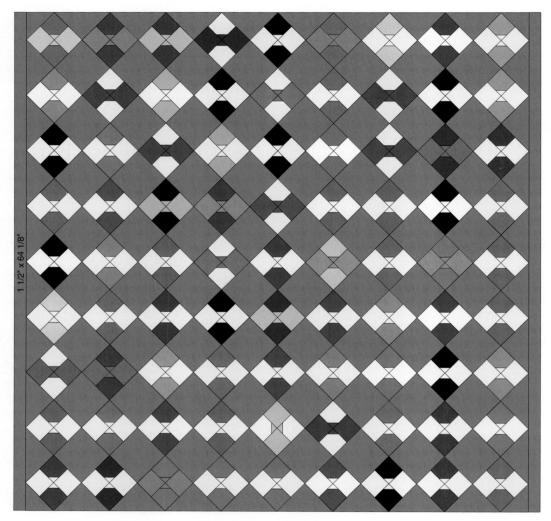

Bow Tie Quilt
Placement Diagram
64 1/8" x 67 1/8"

Instructions

1. To piece one Bow Tie block, cut two squares each 1½" x 1½" and 3" x 3" light scrap and two squares 3" x 3" dark scrap.

2. Draw a line on the wrong side diagonal of each 1½" x 1½" square. Place a square on the corner of the dark scrap squares as shown in Figure 1. Stitch on the marked line, trim seam allowance to ¼" and press open as shown in Figure 2.

3. Join pieced squares in rows with 3" x 3" light scrap squares as shown in Figure 3; join rows to complete one block. Repeat to make 81 blocks.

  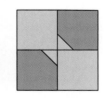

Figure 1
Place a square on the corner of the dark scrap square.

Figure 2
Stitch on marked line; trim seam and press open.

Figure 3
Complete 1 Bow Tie block as shown.

4. Cut two strips 2" x 64⅝" along length of green print; set aside for borders.

5. Cut 11 strips 5½" by remaining fabric width green print; subcut each strip into 5½" setting squares. You will need 64 setting squares.

6. Cut two strips 8⅜" by fabric width green print; subcut into eight squares 8⅜" x 8⅜" and two squares 4½" x 4½". Cut the larger squares on both diagonals to make side triangles and the smaller squares on one diagonal to make corner triangles.

7. Arrange Bow Tie blocks in diagonal rows with setting squares and side triangles as shown in Figure 4; join in rows.

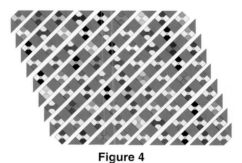

Figure 4
Arrange blocks in diagonal rows with setting squares and side triangles.

8. Join rows and add corner triangles to complete the pieced center.

9. Sew a border strip cut in step 4 to opposite sides of the pieced center to complete the top; press seams toward strips.

10. Sandwich the thin batting with the completed top and prepared backing piece; pin or baste to hold.

Bow Tie

11. Hand- or machine-quilt as desired. *Note: The antique quilt was hand-quilted in the ditch of seams and on diagonals of setting squares using white quilting thread.*

12. Remove pins or basting; trim edges even with top.

13. Bind with self-made or purchased binding to finish.

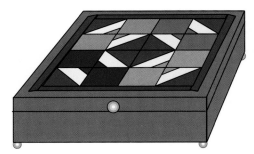

Bow Tie Box
Placement Diagram
7 1/2" x 7 1/2" Design Area

Bow Tie Box

PROJECT Specifications
Design Size: 7½" x 7½"
Block Size: 3¾" x 3¾"
Number of Blocks: 4

Fabric & Batting
- 6" x 6" square each tan, blue, brown and navy prints
- ⅛ yard each cream and green prints
- Thin batting 11" x 11"
- Thick batting 7½" x 7½"

SUPPLIES & TOOLS
- Neutral color all-purpose thread
- Cream quilting thread
- Wooden box with 7½" x 7½" design area
- Craft glue
- Basic tools and supplies, rotary cutter, mat and ruler

Bow Tie Variation
3 3/4" x 3 3/4" Block

Bow Tie Box

Instructions

1. To piece one Bow Tie Variation block, cut one square each green and cream prints 2¾" x 2¾". Draw a line on the wrong side diagonal of the cream print square.

2. Place squares right sides together; sew ¼" from each side of the diagonal line as shown in Figure 5. Cut apart on the marked line; press open to make two triangle/squares.

Figure 5
Sew 1/4" from each side of the diagonal line.

3. Cut two squares each 1⅜" x 1⅜" and 2⅜" x 2⅜" navy print.

4. Draw a line on the wrong side diagonal of the 1⅜" x 1⅜" squares. Place a square right sides together on the cream corner of each triangle/square as shown in Figure 6. Stitch on the marked line, trim seam allowance and press open as shown in Figure 7.

5. Join pieced squares in rows with 2⅜" x 2⅜" navy print squares as shown in Figure 8; join rows to complete one block. Repeat to make four blocks using different print for bow tie in each block.

Figure 6
Place a square on the cream corner of a triangle/square.

Figure 7
Stitch on marked line; trim seam and press open.

Figure 8
Complete 1 Bow Tie Variation block as shown.

6. Join blocks in two rows of two blocks each referring to the Placement Diagram for positioning of blocks. Join rows to complete pieced design.

7. Cut two strips each 1½" x 8" and 1½" x 10" green print. Sew the shorter strips to opposite sides and the longer strips to remaining sides; press seams toward strips.

8. Sandwich the thin batting with the completed top; pin or baste to hold.

9. Quilt as desired by hand or machine. *Note: The sample shown was hand-quilted ¼" from seams in the cream print areas using cream quilting thread.*

10. Remove pins or basting. Trim edges even with pieced top.

11. Cover cardboard insert piece with thick batting square; glue in place.

12. Insert design into box opening as directed in manufacturer's instructions to finish. ❖

Double Wrench

BY SANDRA L. HATCH

There are so many reproduction fabrics available today that it is possible to build a room decor around an antique quilt, and it is almost impossible to tell the old from the new. The pillowcases in the photograph are made from reproduction fabrics; the quilt is antique. Modern quick-piecing techniques are given for both the re-creation of the antique quilt as well as the Double Wrench pillowcases.

Double Wrench

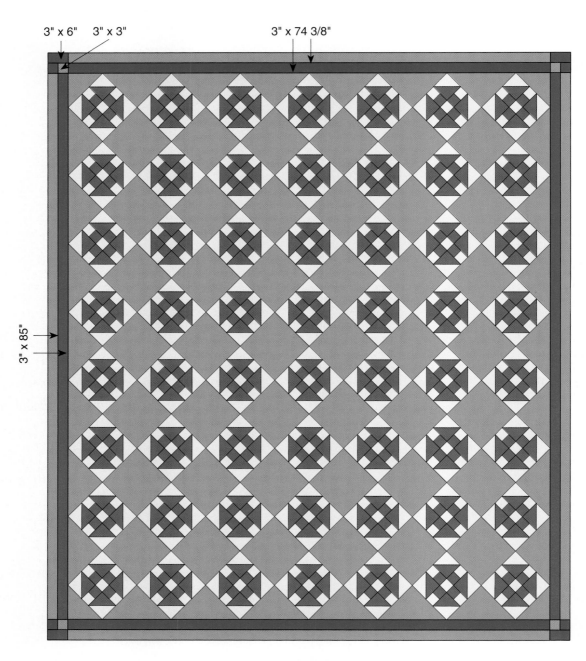

3" x 6" 3" x 3" 3" x 74 3/8"

3" x 85"

Double Wrench Quilt
Placement Diagram
86 3/8" x 97"

Double Wrench Quilt

Double Wrench
7 1/2" x 7 1/2" Block

Project Specifications

Quilt Size: 86⅜" x 97"

Block Size: 7½" x 7½"

Number of Blocks: 56

Fabric & Batting

- 1 yard green print
- 2 yards bittersweet print
- 2½ yards total white shirting prints
- 2¼ yards total brown prints
- Backing 91" x 101"
- Batting 91" x 101"
- 10¾ yards self-made or purchased binding

Supplies & Tools

- Neutral color all-purpose thread
- White quilting thread
- Basic sewing tools and supplies, rotary cutter, mat and ruler

Instructions

1. To make one block, cut two squares each from the same white shirting print and brown print 3⅞" x 3⅞". Cut each square in half on one diagonal to make A triangles. *Note: You may cut three strips each 3⅞" by fabric width from four different white shirting and brown prints and subcut into 3⅞" squares if you will be repeating fabrics and not using scraps.*

2. Cut five squares of the same white shirting print and four squares of the same brown print 2" x 2" for B. *Note: You may cut three 2" by fabric width strips from each fabric noted in step 1 and sew one strip of each fabric together along length to make a strip set. Cut the strip set into 2" segments to make B units as in step 3 if you will be repeating fabrics and not using scraps. Cut another strip each white shirting print; subcut into 2" squares for B.*

3. Sew a white shirting print B to a brown print B; repeat for four B units. Join two B units with a white shirting print B as shown in Figure 1.

Figure 1
Join 2 B units with a
white shirting print B.

Double Wrench

4. Sew a white print A to a brown print A; repeat for four A units.

5. Join two A units with a B unit as shown in Figure 2; repeat for two A-B units.

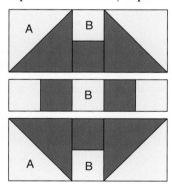

Figure 2
Join 2 A units with a B unit.

6. Join the A-B units with the long B unit as shown in Figure 3 to complete one block; repeat for 56 blocks.

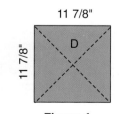

Figure 3
Join the A-B units with the long
B unit to complete 1 block.

7. Cut 48 squares bittersweet print 7½" x 7½" for C.

8. Cut seven squares bittersweet print 11⅞" x 11⅞". Cut each square on both diagonals to make D triangles as shown in Figure 4.

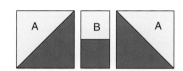

Figure 4
Cut each square on both
diagonals to make D triangles.

9. Cut two squares 6¼" x 6¼" bittersweet print. Cut each square in half on one diagonal to make E triangles.

10. Arrange blocks with C squares and D and E triangles in diagonal rows as shown in Figure 5. Join blocks in rows; join rows to complete pieced center. Press seams in one direction.

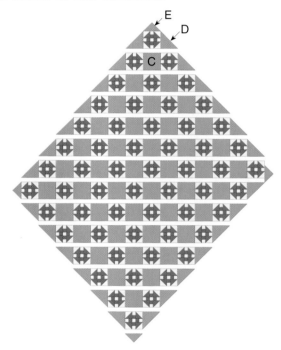

Figure 5
Arrange blocks with C squares and
D and E triangles in diagonal rows.

11. Cut and piece two strips each green print 3½" x 74⅞" and 3½" x 85½". Sew the shorter strips to the top and bottom. Cut four squares bittersweet print 3½" x 3½"; sew a square to each end of the remaining two strips. Sew to opposite long sides; press seams toward strips.

12. Cut and piece two strips each bittersweet print 3½" x 74⅞" and 3½" x 85½". Cut four squares green print 3½" x 3½"; sew a square to each end of the longer strips. Sew the longer strips to opposite long sides of the pieced center. Cut four strips green print 3½" x 6½". Sew a strip to each end of the remaining bittersweet print strips. Sew these strips to the top and bottom of the pieced center; press seams toward strips.

13. Sandwich batting between the completed top and prepared backing piece; pin or baste layers together to hold flat.

14. Quilt as desired by hand or machine. *Note: The quilt shown was hand-quilted in a cross-hatch design on the pieced blocks, diagonal lines spaced 1" apart in the D and E triangles and with a tear-drop design in the C squares using white quilting thread.*

15. When quilting is complete, remove pins or basting; trim edges even. Bind with self-made or purchased binding to complete the quilt.

Double Wrench Pillowcases

Project Specifications

Pillowcase Size: Size Varies

Block Size: 7½" x 7½

Number of Blocks: 10

Fabric & Batting

- ¼ yard green print
- ⅜ yard total brown prints
- Scraps white shirting prints
- ⅓ yard white shirting print
- 2 yards bittersweet print

Supplies & Tools

- Neutral color all-purpose thread
- Basic sewing tools and supplies, rotary cutter, mat and ruler

Double Wrench

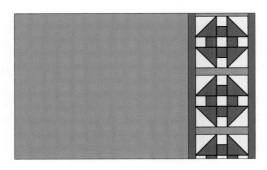

Double Wrench Pillowcase
Placement Diagram
Size Varies

Instructions

1. Complete 10 blocks referring to steps 1–6 for Double Wrench Quilt.

2. Cut two rectangles bittersweet print 28" by fabric width. *Note: Shorter or longer pillowcases are made by varying the length of this strip.*

3. Cut four strips green print 1½" by fabric width for border strips. Cut eight strips bittersweet print 1½" x 8" for sashing. Cut four strips bittersweet print 3" x 8" for end pieces.

4. Join five blocks with four 1½" x 8" sashing strips to make one long strip; sew a 3" x 8" end piece to each end of the strip as shown in Figure 6. Press seams toward strips.

5. Center and sew a green print border strip to each long side of the block strip; press seams toward strips.

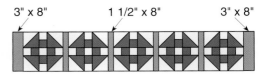

3" x 8"   1 1/2" x 8"   3" x 8"

Figure 6
Join 5 blocks with four 1 1/2" x 8" sashing strips to make 1 long strip; sew a 3" x 8" end piece to each end of the strip as shown.

6. Cut one strip white shirting print 10" by fabric width for lining for pieced section. Press under one long edge ¼".

7. Center and pin unpressed edge of the lining right sides together with the pieced section; stitch. *Note: At this point the ends of the pieced section and the lining may not match.*

8. Press lining and pieced section with seam toward lining piece and topstitch as shown in Figure 7.

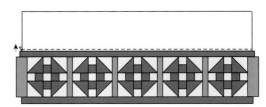

Figure 7
Press lining and pieced section with seam toward lining piece and topstitch as shown.

9. Center and stitch remaining raw edge of the pieced section to one end of one 28"-by-fabric-width rectangle of bittersweet print as shown in Figure 8. *Note: Ends may not match, as shown in Figure 8.*

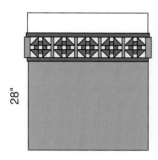

Figure 8
Center and stitch remaining raw
edge of the pieced section to 1 end
of one 28"-by-fabric-width piece of
bittersweet print as shown; ends
may not be even.

10. Trim edges of pieced section even with edges of the bittersweet print unpieced section as shown in Figure 9.

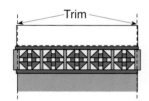

Figure 9
Trim edges of pieced section even
with edges of the bittersweet print
unpieced section.

11. Fold stitched piece with wrong sides together and raw edges even; stitch a ¼" seam. Turn wrong side out; press seam flat.

12. Stitch along the pressed-and-stitched edge with a ⅜" seam allowance to enclose previously stitched seam as shown in Figure 10. *Note: This seam is called a French seam. It is a sturdy seam as there are no raw edges to wear.*

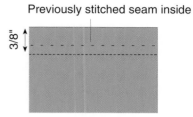

Figure 10
Stitch along the pressed-and-stitched edge
with a 3/8" seam allowance to enclose
previously stitched seam as shown.

13. Fold the lining section to the inside to cover seam where pieced section and bittersweet print sections are joined; baste in place, carefully lining up edges as shown in Figure 11.

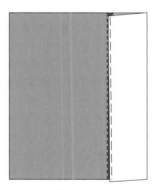

Figure 11
Fold the lining section to the inside to
cover seam where pieced section and
white print pieces are joined; baste in
place, carefully lining up edges as shown.

14. From the right side; topstitch close to seam to catch basted section. Topstitch in the ditch between green print strips and pieced blocks to finish. Repeat for second pillowcase. ❖

Ocean Waves

BY VENUS E. BARDANOUVE

We often do not know the maker of an antique quilt, but we do know who made this one because it has been in the quilter's family for many years. The quiltmaker, Cora Gillispe Potts, came to Nebraska from Iowa in a family wagon train when she was 2 years old. Like many pioneer women in the Midwest, Cora's quilts not only kept her family warm, but also they added touches of beauty to their drab surroundings. Ocean Waves was a popular pattern; it was beautiful either as a planned quilt or a scrap one. Instructions for the traditional method, which Cora probably used to make her quilt, are given here as well as the modern quick-cut method.

Ocean Waves

2" x 64"

2" x 84"

Ocean Waves
Placement Diagram
68" x 84"

Ocean Waves

Project Specifications

Quilt Size: 68" x 84"

Block Size: 16" x 16"

Fabric & Batting

- 3 yards total light blue print
- 3 yards total white print scraps
- 2½ yards white print
- Batting 72" x 88"
- Backing 72" x 88"
- 9¼ yards self-made or purchased binding

Supplies & Tools

- All-purpose thread to match fabrics
- Basic sewing supplies and tools, rotary cutter, mat and ruler

Instructions

Traditional Method

1. Cut and piece two strips white print 2½" x 64½" and two strips 2½" x 84½". Set aside for borders.

2. Prepare templates using pattern pieces given. Cut as directed on each piece for one block and for setting and corner triangles. Repeat for 20 blocks.

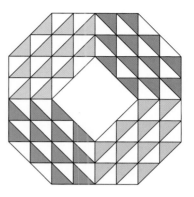

Ocean Waves
16" x 16" Block

3. To piece one block, sew a row of five A triangles beginning and ending with a white print triangle referring to Figure 1; repeat for four units. Sew a row of five A triangles beginning and ending with a blue print triangle; repeat for four units again referring to Figure 1.

Figure 1
Make 4 rows of each version.

4. Sew a row of seven A triangles beginning and ending with a white print triangle referring to Figure 2; repeat for four units. Sew a row of seven A triangles beginning and ending with a blue print triangle again referring to Figure 2; repeat for four units.

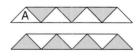

Figure 2
Make 4 rows of each version.

Ocean Waves

5. Join a five-unit row with a seven-unit row; repeat referring to Figure 3. Join these two units; repeat for four units.

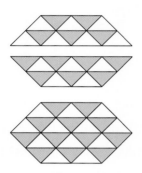

Figure 3
Join a 5-unit row with a 7-unit row; repeat and join.

6. Sew a pieced unit to each side of the B square as shown in Figure 4; repeat for 20 blocks. Press each block.

7. Arrange blocks in five rows of four blocks each as shown in Figure 5. Join the blocks in rows; press.

Figure 4
Sew pieced units to B square.

B

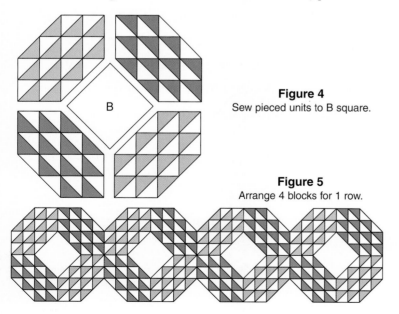

Figure 5
Arrange 4 blocks for 1 row.

8. Join the block rows with B squares referring to Figure 6; press.

9. Set in C triangles on sides and D triangles at the corners to complete the top as shown in Figure 6; press.

Figure 6
Join the block rows with B; set in C and D triangles.

10. Sew the two previously cut 2½" x 64½" white print strips to top and bottom; press seams towards strips. Sew the two 2½" x 84½" white print strips to sides; press seams towards strips.

11. Mark top with desired quilting pattern. The quilt shown was quilted in each block as shown in Figure 7.

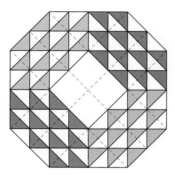

Figure 7
Quilt each block as shown.

12. Sandwich batting between completed top and prepared backing piece. Baste layers together to hold flat.

13. Quilt on marked lines and as desired. When quilting is complete, remove basting. Trim edges even.

14. Bind edges with self-made or purchased binding to finish.

Quicker Method

1. Cut border strips as in step 1 for traditional method.

2. Cut 35 strips white print scraps 2⅞" by fabric width. Layer as many as your rotary cutter will cut through, lining up edges perfectly. Trace template A onto fabric as shown in Figure 8, cutting number needed to complete the quilt. Repeat with blue print strips. You will need 960 of each color triangle to complete quilt.

Figure 8
Trace template on layered strips.

3. Cut six strips white print for B squares 6⅛" by fabric width. Cut each strip into 6⅛" segments. You will need 32 B squares.

4. Cut four squares white print 9¼" x 9¼". Cut each square on both diagonals to make C triangles.

5. Cut two squares 4⅞" x 4⅞" white print. Cut each square on one diagonal to make D triangles.

6. Complete blocks and finish quilt as for traditional methods. ❖

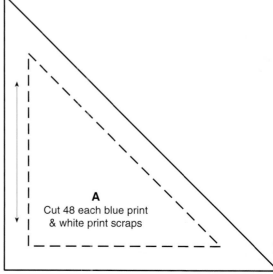

A
Cut 48 each blue print
& white print scraps

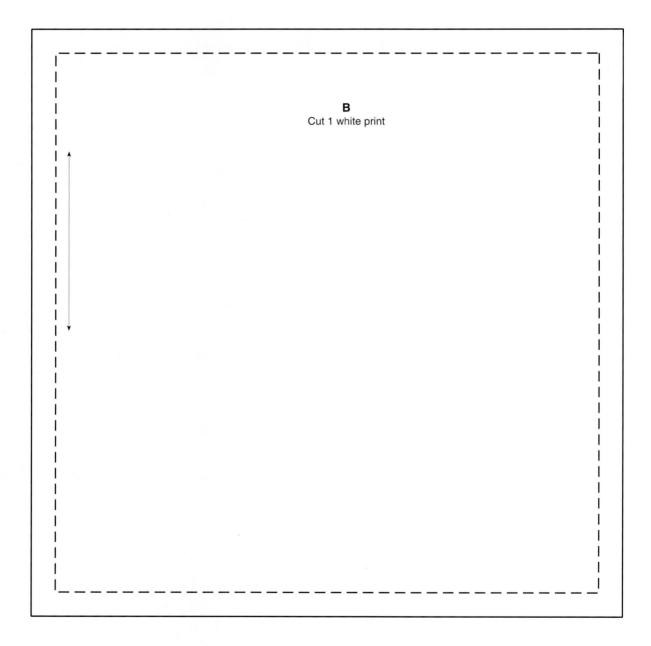

B
Cut 1 white print

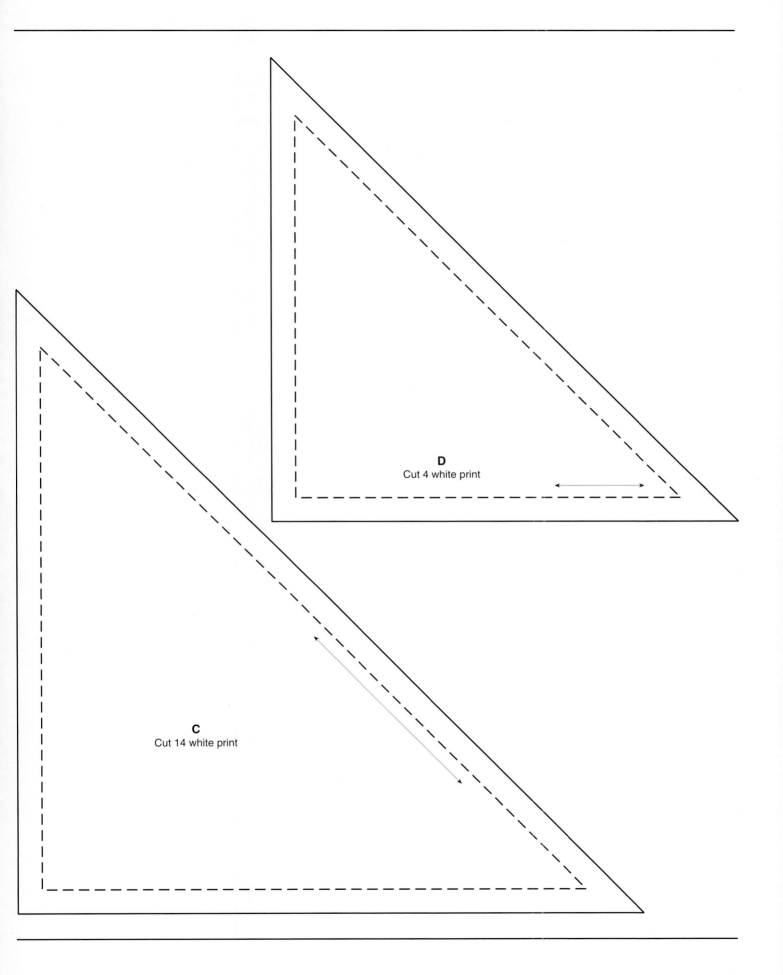

D
Cut 4 white print

C
Cut 14 white print

Lost Children

BY SANDRA L. HATCH

Why this block is named "Lost Children," we'll probably never know. Does it refer to the lost children of Israel in the Bible or to lost children generally? This antique quilt was made using red, white and blue and is heavily quilted. It makes a very pretty quilt in these colors, and you may prefer to give it a happier name when you have finished.

Lost Children

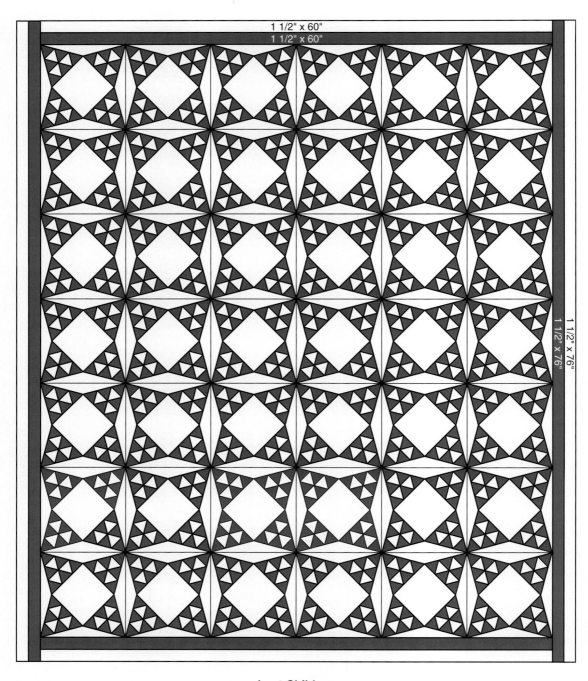

1 1/2" x 60"
1 1/2" x 60"

1 1/2" x 76"
1 1/2" x 76"

Lost Children
Placement Diagram
66" x 76"

Lost Children

Project Specifications

Quilt Size: 66" x 76"

Block Size: 10" x 10"

Number of blocks: 42

Fabric & Batting

- ¾ yard red print
- 4 yards blue print
- 5½ yards white solid
- Batting 70" x 80"
- Backing 70" x 80"
- 8 yards self-made or purchased binding

Supplies & Tools

- 2 spools white all-purpose thread
- White quilting thread
- Basic sewing tools and supplies

Instructions

1. Cut two strips each white solid 2" x 60½" and 2" x 76½"; repeat with blue print to make border strips. Set aside.

2. Prepare templates using pattern pieces given. Cut as directed on each piece to make one block; repeat for 42 blocks.

Lost Children
10" x 10" Block

3. To piece one block, sew two white A pieces to three blue A pieces as shown in Figure 1. Sew one white A piece to two blue A pieces. Join this unit with the previously pieced unit; sew a red A to the narrow end of this unit as shown in Figure 2. Repeat for four units.

Figure 1
Sew 3 blue A pieces together with 2 white A pieces.

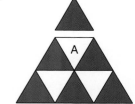

Figure 2
Sew a red A to the narrow end of the pieced unit.

4. Sew a pieced unit to each side of a B square as shown in Figure 3. Set in C pieces on each side as shown in Figure 4 to complete one block; press. Repeat for 42 blocks. ***Note: If you want***

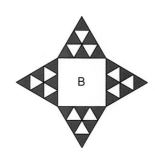

Figure 3
Sew pieced units to each side of B.

Lost Children

to reduce seams, complete units as shown in Figure 3 and use piece D to join pieced units, adding C at ends as needed referring to Figure 5.

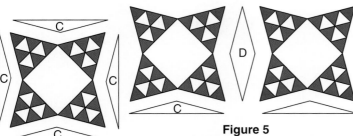

Figure 4
Set in C pieces.

Figure 5
Use piece D to join pieced units instead of making blocks using C. Piece C is used at the ends of each row and at the top and bottom edges and D is used to join all blocks.

5. Join six blocks to make a row; repeat for seven rows. Join rows to complete pieced center; press.

6. Sew a 2" x 60½" blue print strip to a 2" x 60½" white solid strip; press seams toward the blue print strip. Repeat with second set of strips. Sew a pieced strip to the top and bottom of the pieced center with white strips on the outside; press seams toward strips.

7. Sew a 2" x 76½" blue print strip to a 2" x 76½" white solid strip; press seams toward the blue print strip. Repeat with second set of strips. Sew a pieced strip to opposite long sides of the pieced center with white strips on the outside; press seams toward strips.

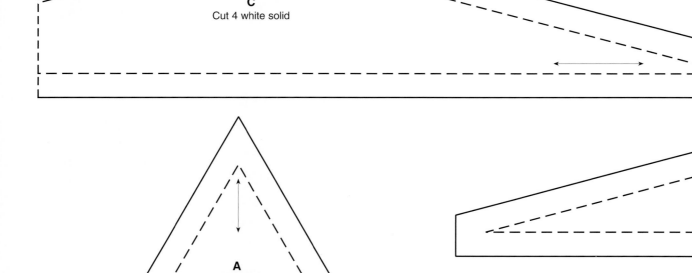

C
Cut 4 white solid

A
Cut 12 white solid, 4 red print & 20 blue print

Join at dotted line on C

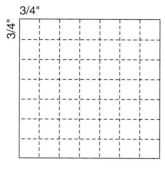

3/4"

3/4"

Figure 6
Mark B squares with
a 3/4" grid as shown.

8. Mark B squares with a ¾" grid as shown in Figure 6.

9. Sandwich batting between completed top and prepared backing piece. Pin or baste layers together.

10. Quilt on marked lines, ¼" from seams of A and C pieces and as desired on borders. When quilting is complete, remove basting or pins; trim edges even.

11. Bind edges with self-made or purchased binding to finish. ❖

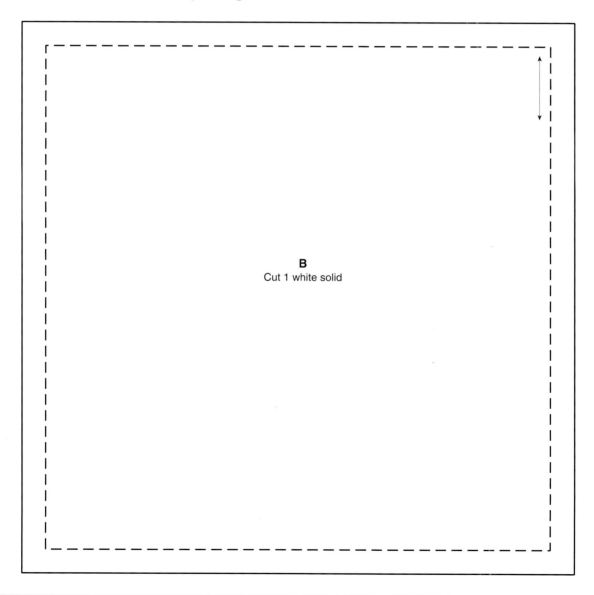

B
Cut 1 white solid

Lost Children

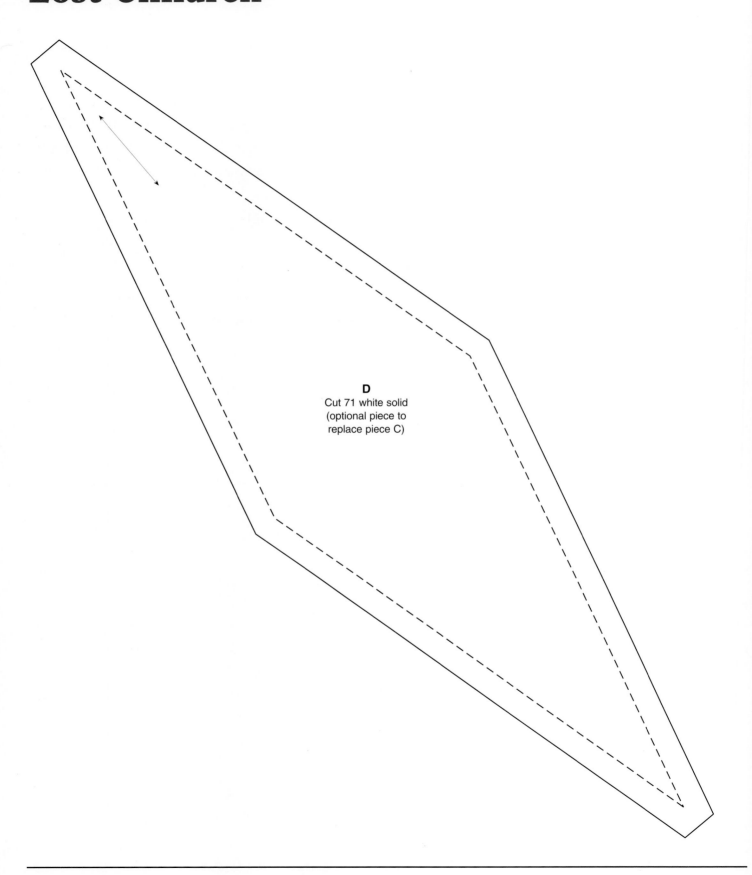

D
Cut 71 white solid
(optional piece to
replace piece C)

Northumberland Star

BY SUE HARVEY

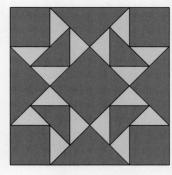

Northumberland Star
7" x 7" Block

The maker of this antique quilt used a number of different green and gold prints to piece the blocks, perhaps using up all her scraps in these colors. Unfortunately, she seems to have run out of green and gold fabric before finishing. The two half blocks on the edge of this quilt, not seen in the photograph, are blue, probably all she had left in her scrap bag. The green and gold fabric and the red print in the outer sashing strips give this late 1880s quilt a festive holiday look. Using some of the reproduction fabrics and the delightful Christmas prints available to us today, you can re-create the quilt or make a table cover for your holiday table.

Northumberland Star Quilt

Project Specifications

Quilt Size: 70⅛" x 89¼"
Block Size: 7" x 7"
Number of Blocks: 65

Fabric & Batting

- ¾ yard red print
- 4 yards gold print
- 4½ yards green print
- Backing 75" x 94"
- Batting 75" x 94"

Supplies & Tools

- Neutral color all-purpose thread
- White quilting thread
- Basic sewing tools and supplies, rotary cutter, mat and ruler

Instructions

1. Cut six strips green print 3" by fabric width; sub-cut five strips into 3" square segments for A and one strip into 1¾" segments for F. You will need 65 A squares and 23 F rectangles.

2. Cut 16 strips green print 2¼" by fabric width;

Northumberland Star

subcut each strip into 2¼" square segments for B. You will need 283 B squares.

3. Cut 10 strips green print 4¾" by fabric width; subcut each strip into 4¾" square segments. Cut each square on both diagonals to make C triangles; you will need 308 C triangles.

4. Cut eight strips green print 3¾" by fabric width; subcut each strip into 3¾" square segments. Cut each square on both diagonals to make D triangles; you will need 333 D triangles.

5. Cut two strips green print 2⅛" by fabric width; subcut each strip into 2⅛" square segments. Cut each square on one diagonal to make E triangles; you will need 50 E triangles.

6. Cut two 1¾" x 1¾" squares green print for G.

7. Cut 31 strips gold print 2⅛" by fabric width; subcut each strip into 2⅛" square segments. Cut each square on one diagonal to make E triangles; you will need 1,232 E triangles.

8. To piece one Northumberland Star block, sew a gold print E to two short sides of D as shown in Figure 1; repeat for four D-E units.

Figure 1
Sew E to 2 short sides of D.

9. Sew a gold print E to two adjacent sides of B as shown in Figure 2; repeat for four B-E units.

Figure 2
Sew E to 2 adjacent sides of B.

10. Sew a B-E unit to a D-E unit as shown in Figure 3; repeat for four B-D units. Sew a B-D unit to opposite sides of A.

Figure 3
Sew B-E to D-E.

11. Sew C to opposite sides of the remaining B-D units as shown in Figure 4. Sew a B-C-D unit to opposite sides of the A-B-D unit to complete one block as shown in Figure 5; repeat to make 65 blocks.

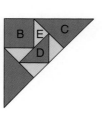

Figure 4
Sew C to opposite sides of B-D

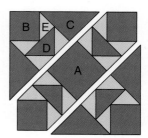

Figure 5
Complete 1 Northumberland Star block as shown.

12. To piece one edge unit, sew a gold print E to two short sides of D. Sew a gold print E to two adjacent sides of B. Join the B-E and D-E units and sew to F as shown in Figure 6.

Figure 6
Sew B-D to F.

13. Sew a gold print E to a green print E along the diagonal; repeat for two E units.

Northumberland Star

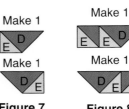

Make 1

Make 1

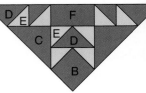

Figure 9
Sew C to 1 side of E-D.

14. Sew a gold print E to D as shown in Figure 7; repeat for two E-D units. Sew an E unit to an E-D unit as shown in Figure 8; repeat for two E-D units.

Make 1

Make 1

Figure 7
Sew E to D.

Figure 8
Sew an E unit to E-D.

15. Sew C to the gold side of each E-D unit as shown in Figure 9; sew a C-E-D unit to opposite sides of the B-D-F unit as shown in Figure 10 to complete one edge unit.

Figure 10
Complete 1 edge unit as shown.

Northumberland Star
Placement Diagram
70 1/8" x 89 1/4"

Repeat to make 23 edge units.

16. To piece one corner unit, make two E-D units referring to steps 13 and 14.

17. Sew G to one E-D unit and C to the remaining E-D unit as shown in Figure 11; join the units to complete one corner unit, again referring to Figure 11. Repeat to make two corner units.

18. Cut four strips green print 2½" by fabric width; subcut each strip into 2½" square segments to make sashing squares. You will need 65 sashing squares.

19. Cut one strip green print 4⅛" by fabric width; subcut into six 4⅛" square segments for I and one 2⅜" square segment for J. Cut each I square on both diagonals and the J square on one diagonal to make triangles; you will need 23 I triangles and two J triangles.

20. Cut three strips red print and seven strips gold print 7½" by fabric width; subcut each strip into 2½" segments to make sashing strips. You will need 46 red and 108 gold sashing strips.

21. Join blocks with edge units and sashing strips to make diagonal block rows as shown in Figure 12.

22. Join sashing strips with I triangles and sashing squares to make sashing rows, again referring to Figure 12.

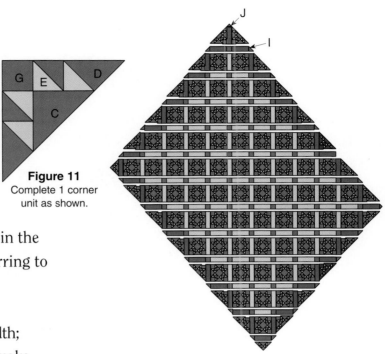

Figure 11
Complete 1 corner
unit as shown.

Figure 12
Complete block and sashing rows as shown.

23. Join the block rows with the sashing rows; add corner units and J triangles to complete the pieced top referring to the Placement Diagram for positioning.

24. Sandwich batting between the prepared backing and completed top; pin or baste to hold.

25. Quilt as desired by hand or machine. *Note: The antique quilt was hand-quilted in diagonal lines through blocks and a 1¼" crosshatch design in the sashing strips using white quilting thread.*

26. Trim backing and batting even with top. Cut nine strips gold print 2½" by fabric width; join strips on short ends to make a long strip. Fold strip in half along length with wrong sides together; press to make binding strip. Bind edges of quilt to finish.

Northumberland Star Table Cover

Project Specifications

Cover Size: 38" x 38"

Block Size: 7" x 7"

Number of Blocks: 12

Fabric & Batting

- ⅜ yard red print
- ¾ yard gold print
- 1¼ yards green print
- Backing 42" x 42"
- Batting 42" x 42"

Supplies & Tools

- All-purpose thread to match fabrics
- Green machine-quilting thread
- Basting spray
- Basic sewing tools and supplies, rotary cutter, mat and ruler

Instructions

1. Cut one strip green print 3" by fabric width; subcut into twelve 3" square segments for A and four 1¾" segments for F.

2. Cut three strips green print 2¼" by fabric width; subcut into 2¼" square segments for B. You will need 52 B squares.

3. Cut two strips green print 4¾" by fabric width; subcut into fourteen 4¾" square segments for C and two 4⅛" square segments for I. Cut C squares and I squares on both diagonals to make triangles; you will need 56 C triangles and eight I triangles.

4. Cut two strips green print 3¾" by fabric width; subcut into fifteen 3¾" square segments for D and four 2⅛" square segments for E. Cut D squares on both diagonals and E squares on one diagonal to make triangles; you will need 60 D and eight E triangles.

5. Cut six strips gold print 2⅛" by fabric width; subcut into 2⅛" square segments. Cut each square on one diagonal to make E triangles; you will need 224 E triangles.

6. Piece 12 Northumberland Star blocks referring to steps 8–11 for Northumberland Quilt and four edge units referring to steps 12–15 for Northumberland Quilt.

7. Cut one strip green print 2½" by fabric width; subcut into 2½" square segments to make sashing squares. You will need 13 sashing squares.

8. Cut one strip each red and gold prints 7½" by fabric width; subcut each strip into 2½" segments for sashing strips. You will need 16 strips each red and gold prints.

9. Join two blocks with two edge units and one gold print and two red print sashing strips to make a row as shown in Figure 13; repeat for two rows.

10. Join four blocks with two red print and three gold print sashing strips to make a row, again referring to Figure 13; repeat for two rows.

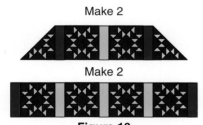

Make 2

Make 2

Figure 13
Complete block rows as shown.

11. Join sashing strips with sashing squares and I triangles to make sashing rows as shown in Figure 14.

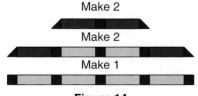

Make 2

Make 2

Make 1

Figure 14
Complete sashing rows as shown.

12. Join block rows with sashing rows to complete

Northumberland Star Table Cover
Placement Diagram
38" x 38"

the pieced top referring to the Placement Diagram for positioning of rows.

13. Apply basting spray to one side of batting; place wrong side of prepared backing piece against sprayed side. Repeat with completed top on remaining side of batting.

14. Quilt as desired by hand or machine. *Note: The sample shown was machine-quilted in diagonal lines through the blocks and sashing using green machine-quilting thread in the top of the machine and all-purpose thread in the bobbin.*

15. Trim backing and batting even with the quilted top. Cut four strips green print 2¼" by fabric width; join strips on short ends to make a long strip. Fold strip in half along length with wrong sides together; press to make binding strip. Bind edges of table cover to finish. ❖

Broken Dishes

BY SANDRA L. HATCH

It's easy to tell why the pioneer quiltmaker gave this name to her quilt; the many scraps must have reminded her of pieces of broken dishes. Using quick methods and lots of scraps, this quilt is very easy to duplicate.

Broken Dishes

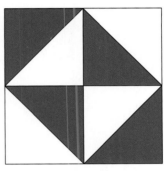

Broken Dishes
7" x 7" Block

Project Specifications

Quilt Size: 63" x 77"

Block Size: 7" x 7"

Number of Blocks: 50

Fabric & Batting

- 100 scrap squares 4⅜" x 4⅜" (cut 2 squares of same scrap for each block)
- 4 yards white solid
- Backing 67" x 81"
- Batting 67" x 81"
- 8¼ yards self-made or purchased binding

Supplies & Tools

- White all-purpose thread
- White quilting thread
- Basic sewing tools and supplies, rotary cutter, mat and ruler

Instructions

1. Cut each scrap square in half on one diagonal to make triangles; you will need four triangles for each block. Set aside.

2. Cut 12 strips white solid 4⅜" by fabric width. Cut strips into 4⅜" square segments. You will need 100 squares. Cut each square in half on one diagonal to make triangles.

3. Sew a scrap triangle to a white solid triangle to make a square; repeat for four triangles from the same scrap. Join the triangle/squares as shown in Figure 1 to make one block. Repeat for 50 blocks.

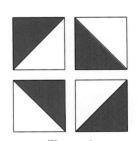

Figure 1
Join triangle/squares
to complete 1 block.

4. Cut 10 strips white solid 7½" by fabric width. Cut strips into 7½" square segments. You will need 49 squares.

Broken Dishes

Broken Dishes
Placement Diagram
63" x 77"

5. Join five pieced blocks with four white solid squares to make a row as shown in Figure 2; repeat for six rows, arranging blocks in random direction or in a planned arrangement. *Note: The quilt shown* *seems to have a random placement. The appearance of the quilt changes if all blocks face the same direction as shown in Figure 3 or if every other block is turned as shown in Figure 4.*

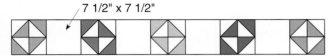

Figure 2
Join 5 pieced blocks with 4 white solid squares to make a row.

Figure 3
The quilt takes on a different look when blocks are arranged all in one direction.

Figure 4
Alternate the direction of blocks to create a different look.

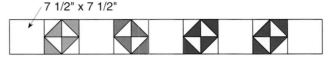

Figure 5
Join 4 pieced blocks with 5 white solid squares to make a row.

6. Join four pieced blocks with five white solid squares to make a row as shown in Figure 5; repeat for five rows, arranging blocks in random direction or a planned arrangement as in step 5.

7. Join rows to complete pieced center beginning and ending with a five pieced-block row; press.

8. Mark white solid squares with a chosen quilting design.

9. Sandwich batting between completed top and prepared backing piece. Pin or baste layers together to hold flat.

10. Quilt as desired by hand or machine. When quilting is complete, remove pins or basting. Trim edges even.

11. Bind with self-made or purchased binding to finish. ❖

Migrating Geese

BY SANDRA L. HATCH

More than 100 years ago the colors in this beautiful quilt were probably as vibrant as the colors in the reproduction fabrics used to make the table runner. Wear and fabric deterioration have taken their toll, but it doesn't take much imagination to visualize the beauty of the antique quilt with the yellow/ green and brown prints as they were originally. Many old-time quilters left blocks off the top of a quilt to make it easier to fit on a bed. This quiltmaker left only one block off one side. We show the Placement Diagram with both corner blocks missing. If you want to make the quilt square, make two more blocks.

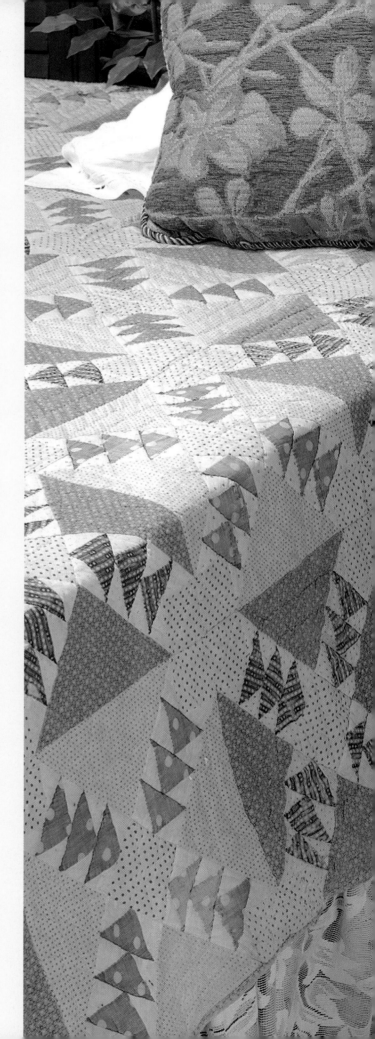

Migrating Geese

Migrating Geese
Placement Diagram
76 1/2" x 89 1/4"

Migrating Geese Quilt

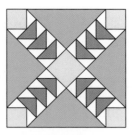

Yellow/Green Migrating Geese
12 3/4" x 12 3/4" Block

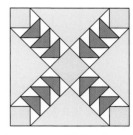

Cream Migrating Geese
12 3/4" x 12 3/4" Block

Project Specifications

Quilt Size: 76½" x 89¼"

Block Size: 12¾" x 12¾"

Number of Blocks: 40

Fabric & Batting

- 1¼ yards cream-with-red dots
- 1½ yards cream-with-green pin dot
- 1½ yards yellow/green print
- 2½ yards total brown and green prints
- 4 yards total shirting prints and cream solid
- Backing 80" x 93"
- Batting 80" x 93"
- 9¾ yards self-made or purchased binding

Supplies & Tools

- Neutral color all-purpose thread
- Cream quilting thread
- Basic sewing tools and supplies, rotary cutter, mat and ruler

Instructions

1. Cut five strips cream-with-green pin dot 9¾" by fabric width; subcut into 9¾" square segments. Cut each on both diagonals to make A triangles as shown in Figure 1. You will need 80 cream-with-green pin dot A triangles. Repeat with five strips yellow/green print to make 80 yellow/green print A triangles.

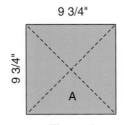

9 3/4"

9 3/4"

A

Figure 1
Cut on both diagonals
to make A triangles.

2. Cut four strips cream-with-red dot 3½" by fabric width; subcut into 3½" square segments for B. You will need 40 B squares.

3. Cut 10 strips cream-with-red dot 2⅝" by fabric width; subcut into 2⅝" square segments for C. You will need 160 C squares.

4. Cut 12 rectangles brown or green print 2" x 3½" for D in each block or a total of 480 D rectangles. *Note: If using strips, you will need 23 strips 3½" by fabric width; subcut into 2" segments.*

5. Cut 24 squares shirting prints or cream solid 2" x 2" for E in each block or a total of 960 E squares. *Note: If using strips you will need 46 strips 2" by fabric width.*

6. Cut four squares shirting prints or cream solid 2⅜" x 2⅜" for F in each block or a total of 160 squares. Cut each square on one diagonal to make a total of 320 F triangles. *Note: If using strips, you will need 12 strips 2⅜" by fabric width.*

Migrating Geese

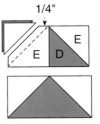

Figure 6
Repeat with a second E on
the adjacent corner to
complete 1 Flying Geese unit.

7. To make a Flying Geese unit, lay E right sides together with D as shown in Figure 2.

Figure 2
Lay E right sides
together with D.

8. Sew on one diagonal as shown in Figure 3. Trim ¼" from stitching line as shown in Figure 4.

Figure 3
Sew on 1 diagonal.

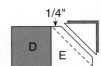

Figure 4
Trim 1/4" from stitching line.

9. Press stitched unit as shown in Figure 5. Repeat with a second E on the adjacent corner as shown in Figure 6 to complete one Flying Geese unit. Repeat for 12 units for each block or a total of 480 units for quilt shown.

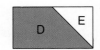

Figure 5
Press stitched unit.

10. Sew an F triangle to two adjacent corners of a C square as shown in Figure 7; repeat for four corner units per block or a total of 160 corner units for quilt shown.

Figure 7
Sew an F triangle to 2
adjacent corners of a
C square to complete
a corner unit.

11. Join three Flying Geese units with a corner unit as shown in Figure 8; repeat for four D-F-C units. Sew a cream-with-green pin dot A to each side of each unit as shown in Figure 9.

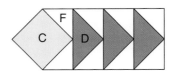

Figure 8
Join 3 Flying Geese
units with a corner unit.

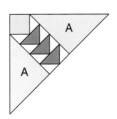

Figure 9
Sew a cream-with-green pin dot
A to each side of each unit.

12. Sew a D-F-C unit to two opposite sides of B as shown in Figure 10.

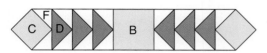

Figure 10
Sew a D-F-C unit to 2 opposite sides of B.

13. Join the pieced units as shown in Figure 11 to complete one cream block; repeat for 20 cream blocks.

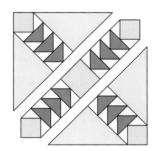

Figure 11
Join the pieced units as shown
to complete 1 cream block.

14. Repeat steps 11 and 12 using yellow/green A pieces as shown in Figure 12 to complete 20 yellow/green blocks.

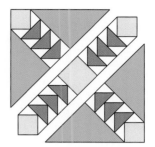

Figure 12
Join the pieced units as shown to
complete 1 yellow/green block.

15. Join three yellow/green blocks with three cream blocks to complete a row; repeat for six rows. Join rows to make a square section. Join two yellow/green blocks with two cream blocks to make a row. Sew to one end of the stitched section to complete the pieced top referring to the Placement Diagram for positioning of blocks.

16. Sandwich batting between completed top and prepared backing piece; pin or baste layers together to hold flat.

17. Quilt in the ditch of seams or as desired by hand or machine using cream quilting thread.

18. When quilting is complete, remove pins or basting. Bind edges with self-made or purchased binding to finish.

Migrating Geese Table Runner

Project Specifications

Runner Size: 18¾" x 63"

Block Size: 12¾" x 12¾"

Number of Blocks: 3

Fabric & Batting

- Scraps of 3 brown reproduction prints
- ¼ yard tan pin dot
- ⅜ yard cream solid
- ⅜ yard brown floral print
- ⅝ yard yellow/green print
- Backing 23" x 67"
- Batting 23" x 67"
- 3¼ yards self-made or purchased binding

Supplies & Tools

- Neutral color all-purpose thread
- Clear nylon monofilament
- Basic sewing tools and supplies, rotary cutter, mat and ruler

Instructions

1. Cut four strips 2" by fabric width cream solid; subcut each strip into 2" segments for E squares. You will need 72 E squares.

2. Cut one strip each 3½" by fabric width three different brown prints; subcut each strip into 2" segments for D. You will need 12 D rectangles of each print.

3. Cut one strip 2⅜" by fabric width cream solid; subcut strip into 2⅜" square segments for E. Cut each square in half on one diagonal for F. You will need 24 F triangles.

4. Cut one strip 2⅝" by fabric width tan pin dot; subcut strip into 2⅝" squares for C. You will need 12 C squares.

5. Cut one strip 3½" by fabric width tan pin dot; subcut strip into 3½" square segments for B. You will need 7 B squares.

6. Cut three 9¾" x 9¾" squares yellow/green print. Cut each square on both diagonals to make 12 A triangles.

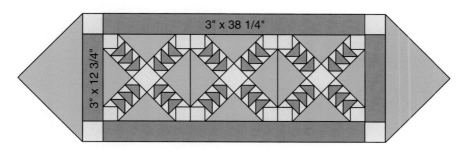

Migrating Geese Table Runner
Placement Diagram
18 3/4" x 63"

7. Complete three yellow/green Migrating Geese blocks referring to steps 7–12 for Migrating Geese Quilt.

8. Join the three blocks to make a row; press seams in one direction.

9. Cut two strips each 3½" x 13¼" and 3½" x 38¾" brown floral print. Sew the longer strips to opposite long sides of the pieced center; press seams toward strips.

10. Sew a B square to each end of the 3½" x 13¼" strips; press seams toward strips. Sew a strip to opposite ends of the pieced center; press seams toward strips.

11. Cut one 14¼" x 14¼" square yellow/green print. Cut the square on one diagonal to make the end triangles. Sew a triangle on each end of the pieced center to complete the runner top.

12. Prepare runner for quilting and finish referring to steps 16–18 for Migrating Geese Quilt. *Note: The runner shown was machine-quilted in the ditch of seams and in a meandering design using clear nylon monofilament in the top of the machine and all-purpose thread in the bobbin.* ❖

Double Pink Kaleidoscope

BY ALEX DUPRE

Kaleidoscope quilts have always been popular because with a simple block arrangement, the quilter gets so much motion. Today, we'd call this "Op Art" and make plans to show our results in the modern museum. Using the reproduction prints currently on the market, you can create a quilt that looks just like its antique version but is still graphically exciting.

Double Pink Kaleidoscope

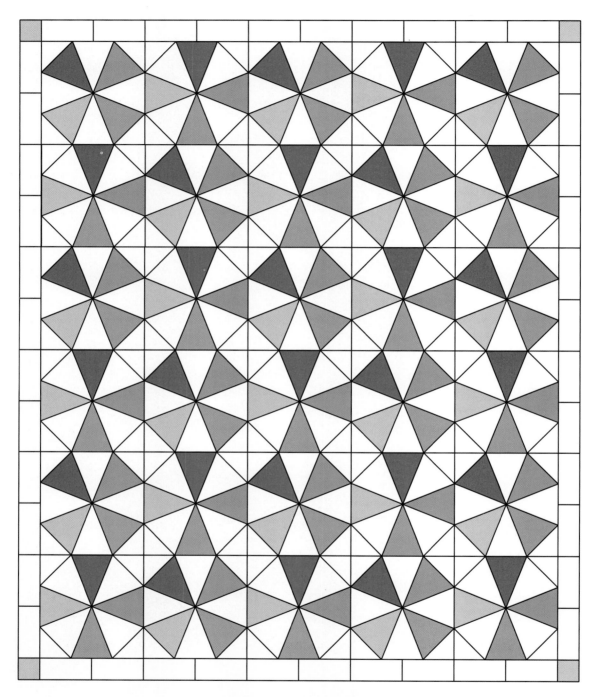

Double Pink Kaleidoscope
Placement Diagram
56" x 66"

Double Pink Kaleidoscope

Project Specifications

Project Size: 56" x 66"

Block Size: 10" x 10"

Number of Blocks: 30

Fabric & Batting

- ⅜ yard each 8 pink prints
- ½ yard each 8 white prints
- Backing 60" x 70"
- Batting 60" x 70"
- 7¼ yards self-made or purchased binding

Supplies & Tools

- All-purpose thread to match fabrics
- Off-white quilting thread
- Basic sewing tools and supplies, rotary cutter, mat and ruler

Instructions

1. Prepare templates using pattern pieces given; cut as directed on each piece for one block and borders. Repeat for 30 blocks.

2. Sew a white print B to a pink print C as shown in Figure 1; repeat for four B-C units. Join the units as shown in Figure 2; press.

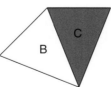

Figure 1
Sew a white print
B to a pink print C.

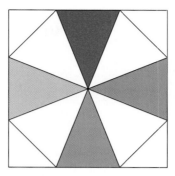 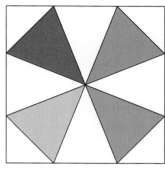

Double Pink Kaleidoscope A
10" x 10" Block

Double Pink Kaleidoscope B
10" x 10" Block

3. Sew A to each corner to complete one A block as shown in Figure 2; press. Repeat for 15 A blocks.

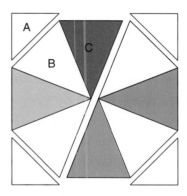

Figure 2
Join the units as shown
to make A blocks.

4. Repeat with pink print B and white print C pieces as shown in Figure 3 to make 15 B blocks.

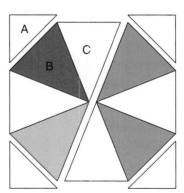

Figure 3
Join pink print B and white print
C pieces to make B blocks.

Double Pink Kaleidoscope

5. Join three A blocks with two B blocks to make a row as shown in Figure 4; repeat for three rows. Press seams in one direction.

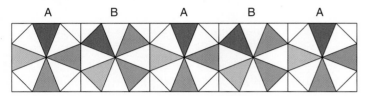

Figure 4
Join 3 A blocks with 2 B blocks to make a row.

6. Join three B blocks with two A blocks to make a row as shown in Figure 5; repeat for three rows. Press seams in one direction.

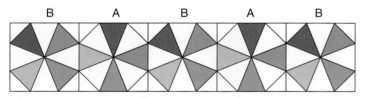

Figure 5
Join 3 B blocks with 2 A blocks to make a row.

7. Join the rows referring to the Placement Diagram; press seams in one direction.

8. Join 12 D pieces on the short ends to make a border strip as shown in Figure 6; press seams in one direction. Repeat for two strips. Sew a strip to two opposite long sides of the pieced center; press seams toward pieced strips.

Figure 6
Join 12 D pieces on the short ends to make a border strip.

9. Join 10 D pieces on the short ends to make a border strip; press seams in one direction. Repeat for two strips. Sew an E square to each end of each strip as shown in Figure 7. Sew a strip to the top and bottom of the pieced center; press seams toward pieced strips.

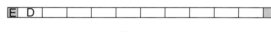

Figure 7
Sew an E square to each end of each strip.

10. Sandwich batting between completed top and prepared backing piece; pin or baste layers together to hold flat.

11. Quilt as desired by hand or machine. *Note: The quilt shown was machine-quilted in the ditch of all seams. When quilting is complete, remove pins or basting; trim edges even.*

12. Bind edges with self-made or purchased binding to finish. ❖

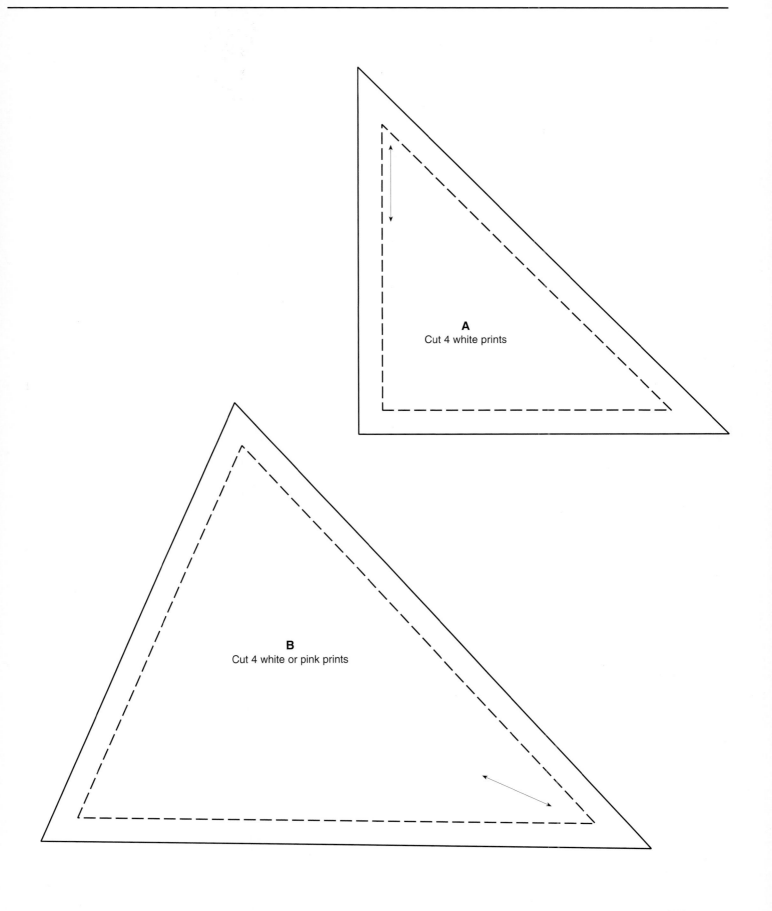

A
Cut 4 white prints

B
Cut 4 white or pink prints

Double Pink Kaleidoscope

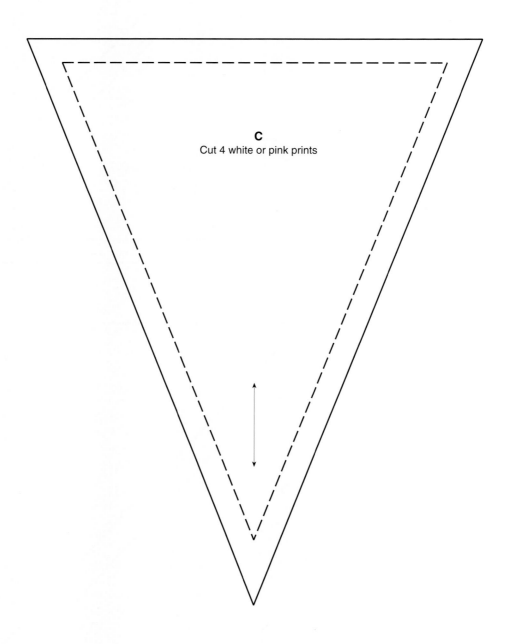

C
Cut 4 white or pink prints

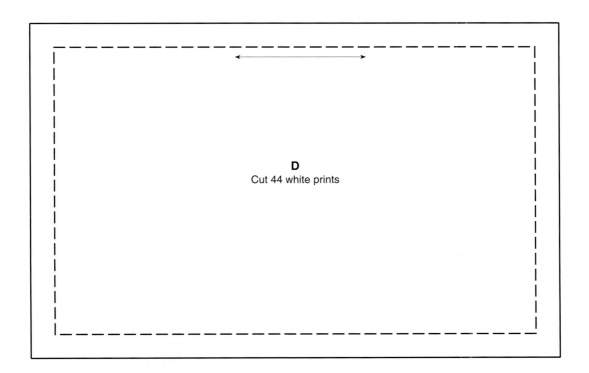

D
Cut 44 white prints

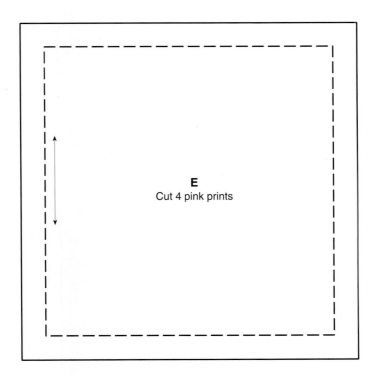

E
Cut 4 pink prints

Mother's Handkerchiefs

BY NORMA PFISTER

Years ago, before the days of paper tissues, everyone had a stash of handkerchiefs. Many of them were wonderful reminders of people or events. This quilter decided to remember those occasions by turning her handkerchiefs into butterflies and putting them into a quilt. If you have some pretty handkerchiefs on hand, or if you can find some at yard sales or flea markets, you too can re-create this charming quilt.

Mother's Handkerchief

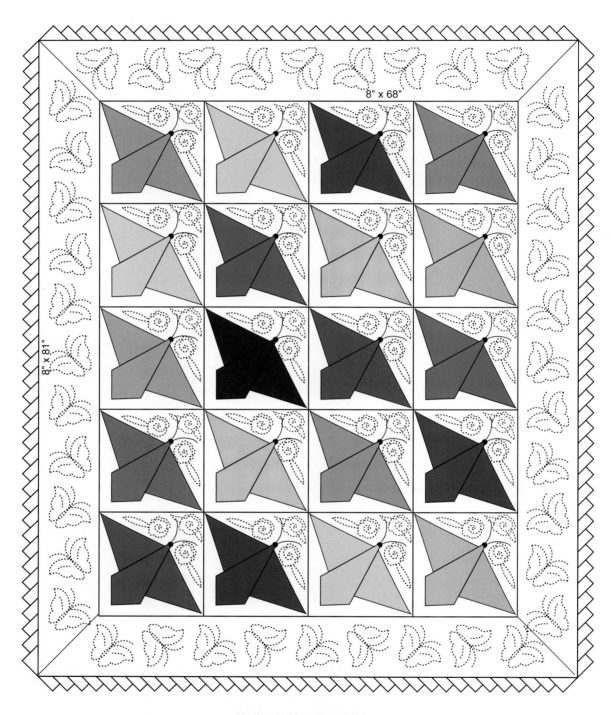

Mother's Handkerchiefs
Placement Diagram
68" x 81"

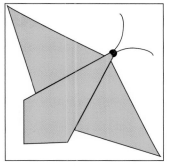

Mother's Handkerchiefs
13" x 13" Block

Mother's Handkerchiefs

Project Specifications

Quilt Size: 68" x 81"

Block Size: 13" x 13"

Number of Blocks: 20

Fabric & Batting

- 20 handkerchiefs (try to find some all the same size)
- 6 yards white for background blocks, borders and prairie-point edge
- Backing 72" x 85"
- Batting 72" x 85"

Supplies & Tools

- Neutral color all-purpose thread
- Various colors of embroidery floss to match handkerchiefs
- Basic sewing tools and supplies, water-erasable fabric marker

Instructions

1. Cut 20 background blocks 13½" x 13½". Fold each block crosswise twice and crease to mark center lines. These lines will be the guides to sew the hankies onto the block. The point on the bottom of the wings should be on the cross-fold lines and the butterfly's head is located a little beyond the center on the opposite fold line referring to Figure 1.

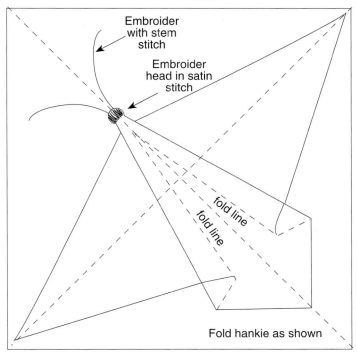

Embroider with stem stitch

Embroider head in satin stitch

fold line

fold line

Fold hankie as shown

Figure 1
Fold hankies and place on background block as shown.

2. Fold the hankie crosswise, keeping the top hem slightly over the bottom hem. Pin or baste the edges together.

3. Bring a folding pleat toward the center on both sides, overlapping about 1" on the bottom and ½" at the top. Both sides should have the same size tucks. This makes the wings of the butterfly angle away from the head. The tip of the wing should touch on the fold line out nearest the edge of the block. The

Mother's Handkerchief

hankie should not go out to the seam line of the block. The pleat forms the butterfly's body and tail.

4. When you have a pleasing shape, pin in place and press lightly with an iron. Do not stretch the hankie in this process.

5. When the hankies have been folded, positioned and basted in place, appliqué down with embroidery floss matching the outer stitched edge of the hankie.

6. Stitch up the pleated section to hold in place using a buttonhole or other stitch that shows on the top of the work. Stitches should be evenly spaced and neat.

7. After the shape has been securely appliquéd in place, embroider a pointed head shape and antennae on each butterfly to complete. Repeat for 20 blocks.

8. Sew the blocks in four rows of five blocks each. Join the rows to complete the center section of the quilt; press.

9. Cut two border strips from white 8½" x 68½"; stitch to the top and bottom. Cut two more strips 8½" x 81½"; stitch to each side, mitering corners. Press seams toward strips.

10. Mark quilt top with the quilting patterns given using water-erasable marker or pencil.

11. Sandwich batting between completed top and prepared backing. Quilt as desired and on marked lines. Stop quilting stitches at least ½" from edge if prairie points will be added to outside edges.

12. Trim batting and backing even with top.

13. To add prairie points, cut 4" x 4" squares from white fabric. You will need at least 170 squares to finish around the edge of the quilt.

14. Fold each square twice diagonally to result in a triangle with one raw edge as shown in Figure 2. Sew the triangles together in a line, overlapping approximately one-third of the previous triangle. When you have a line long enough to fit on one side, pin it to the quilt top with the top side of the triangle against the sides of the quilt.

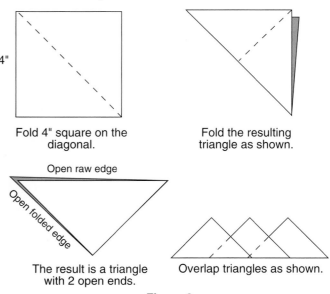

4"

Fold 4" square on the diagonal.

Fold the resulting triangle as shown.

Open raw edge

Open folded edge

The result is a triangle with 2 open ends.

Overlap triangles as shown.

Figure 2
Make prairie-point border sections as shown.

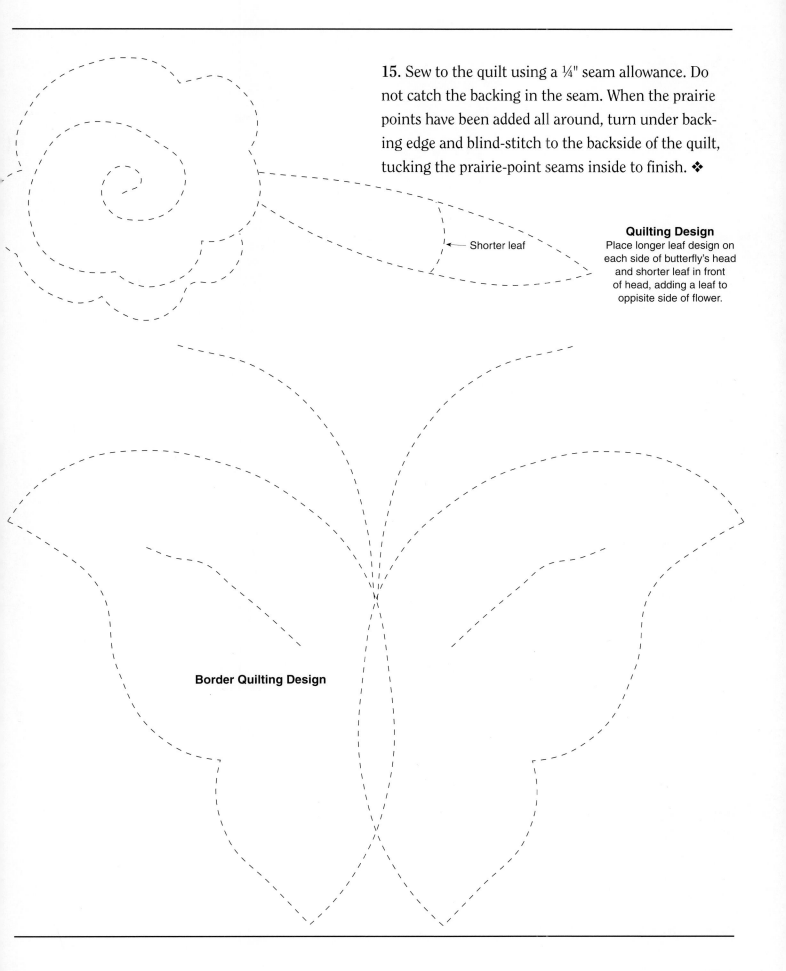

15. Sew to the quilt using a ¼" seam allowance. Do not catch the backing in the seam. When the prairie points have been added all around, turn under backing edge and blind-stitch to the backside of the quilt, tucking the prairie-point seams inside to finish. ❖

← Shorter leaf

Quilting Design
Place longer leaf design on each side of butterfly's head and shorter leaf in front of head, adding a leaf to oppisite side of flower.

Border Quilting Design

Postage Stamp

BY CAROL SCHERER

This quilt is a fascinating attempt to create order out of chaos. The pattern used to create the quilt uses variations of the Snowball and the Five-Patch blocks with over 4,500 pieces. With modern quick-piecing methods, this is a manageable project, but it is mind-boggling to imagine the work of the quilter who methodically pieced this quilt years ago.

 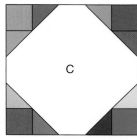

Five-Patch
5" x 5" Block

Postage Stamp Snowball
5" x 5" Block

Project Specifications

Quilt Size: 75" x 90"

Block Size: 5" x 5"

Fabric & Batting

- Variety of strips of fabric 1½" and 1⅞" by any width
- 3¾ yards muslin
- Backing 79" x 94"
- Batting 79" x 94"
- 9¾ yards self-made or purchased binding

Supplies & Tools

- Neutral color all-purpose thread
- Basic sewing supplies and tools, rotary cutter, mat and ruler

Instructions

1. Cut two strips muslin 3" x 75½" and two strips 3" x 90½"; set aside.

2. To make the Five-Patch block, join 1½" scrap strips in groups of five; press. Cut each strip set in 1½" segments as shown in Figure 1.

1 1/2"

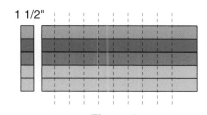

Figure 1
Sew 5 strips together; cut into 1 1/2" segments.

3. Join five segments to make one block; repeat for 119 blocks and press. *Note: For those who prefer to rotary-cut 1½" x 1½" squares of a variety of prints, cut 25 squares for each block or 2,975 squares.*

Postage Stamp

2 1/2" x 75"

2 1/2" x 90"

Postage Stamp
Placement Diagram
75" x 90"

4. For the Snowball block, cut four 1½" x 1½" squares for A and four 1⅞" x 1⅞" squares from scraps. Cut the 1⅞" x 1⅞" squares in half on the diagonal to make two B triangles from each square. *Note: For a real scrap look, cut 476 squares 1⅞" x 1⅞"; cut in half on the diagonal and mix and match in all blocks.*

5. Sew B to adjacent sides of A as shown in Figure 2; repeat for four units. Cut 119 squares 5½" x 5½" from remaining muslin for C or use C template for exact pattern. Sew a pieced unit to each corner of the C square, trimming away

Figure 2
Sew 2 B triangles to an A square.

excess under pieced unit after stitching; press. Repeat for 119 blocks.

6. Arrange the pieced Five-Patch blocks with the Snowball blocks in rows referring to Figure 3. Join in rows; press.

Make 9 rows

Make 8 rows

Figure 3
Arrrange the pieced blocks in rows as shown.

7. Arrange the rows referring to the Placement Diagram. Join in rows; press.

8. Sew the 3" x 75½" strips to the top and bottom and 3" x 90½" strips to sides of quilt, mitering corners. *Note: The antique version has two plain borders and two pieced borders. The pieced borders do not add anything to the design quality of the quilt, so instructions are not given for piecing borders.*

9. Mark top for quilting as desired.

10. Sandwich batting between the completed top and prepared backing piece. Pin or baste layers together.

11. Quilt as desired by hand or machine. When quilting is complete, trim edges even. Remove pins or basting.

12. Bind edges with self-made or purchased binding to finish. ❖

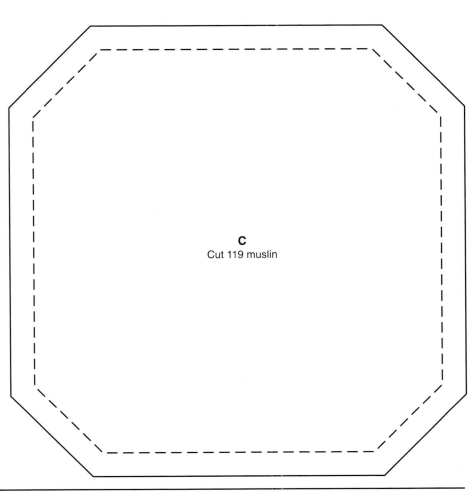

C
Cut 119 muslin

General Instructions

Quiltmaking Basics

Materials & Supplies

Fabrics

Fabric Choices. Quilts and quilted projects combine fabrics of many types. Use same-fiber-content fabrics when making quilted items, if possible.

Buying Fabrics. One hundred percent cotton fabrics are recommended for making quilts. Choose colors similar to those used in the quilts shown or colors of your own preference. Most quilt designs depend more on contrast of values than on the colors used to create the design.

Preparing the Fabric for Use. Fabrics may be prewashed depending on your preference. Whether you prewash or not, be sure your fabrics are colorfast and won't run onto each other when washed after use.

Fabric Grain. Fabrics are woven with threads going in a crosswise and lengthwise direction. The threads cross at right angles—the more threads per inch, the stronger the fabric.

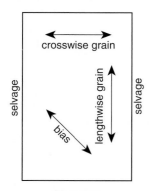

Figure 1
Drawing shows lengthwise, crosswise and bias threads.

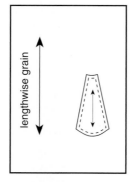

Figure 2
Place the template with marked arrow on the lengthwise grain of the fabric.

The crosswise threads will stretch a little. The lengthwise threads will not stretch at all. Cutting the fabric at a 45-degree angle to the crosswise and lengthwise threads produces a bias edge which stretches a great deal when pulled (Figure 1).

If templates are given with patterns in this book, pay careful attention to the grain lines marked with arrows. These arrows indicate that the piece should be placed on the lengthwise grain with the arrow running on one thread. Although it is not necessary to examine the fabric and find a thread to match to, it is important to try to place the arrow with the lengthwise grain of the fabric (Figure 2).

Thread

For most piecing, good-quality cotton or cotton-covered polyester is the thread of choice. Inexpensive polyester threads are not recommended because they can cut the fibers of cotton fabrics.

Choose a color thread that will match or blend with the fabrics in your quilt. For projects pieced with dark and light color fabrics choose a neutral thread color, such as a medium gray, as a compromise between colors. Test by pulling a sample seam.

Batting

Batting is the material used to give a quilt loft or thickness. It also adds warmth.

Batting size is listed in inches for each pattern to reflect the size needed to complete the quilt according to the instructions. Purchase the size large enough to cut the size you need for the quilt of your choice.

Some qualities to look for in batting are drapability, resistance to fiber migration, loft and softness.

Tools & Equipment

There are few truly essential tools and little equipment required for quiltmaking. Basics include needles (hand-sewing and quilting betweens), pins (long, thin, sharp pins are best), sharp scissors or shears, a thimble, template materials (plastic or cardboard), marking tools (chalk marker, water-erasable pen and a No. 2 pencil are a few) and a quilting frame or hoop. For piecing and/or quilting by machine, add a sewing machine to the list.

Other sewing basics such as a seam ripper, pincushion, measuring tape and an iron are also necessary. For choosing colors or quilting designs for your quilt, or for designing your own quilt, it is helpful to have on hand graph paper, tracing paper, colored pencils or markers and a ruler.

For making strip-pieced quilts, a rotary cutter, mat and specialty rulers are often used. We recommend an ergonomic rotary cutter, a large self-healing mat and several rulers. If you can choose only one size, a 6" x 24" marked in ⅛" or ¼" increments is recommended.

Construction Methods

Traditional Templates. While some quilt instructions in this book use rotary-cut strips and quick sewing methods, many patterns require a template. Templates are like the pattern pieces used to sew a garment. They are used to cut the fabric pieces that make up the quilt top. There are two types—templates that include a ¼" seam allowance and those that don't.

Choose the template material and the pattern. Transfer the pattern shapes to the template material with a sharp No. 2 lead pencil. Write the pattern name, piece letter or number, grain line and number to cut for one block or whole quilt on each piece as shown in Figure 3.

Some patterns require a reversed piece (Figure 4). These patterns are labeled with an R after the piece letter; for example, B and BR. To reverse a template, first cut it with the labeled side up and then with the labeled side down. Compare these to the right and left fronts of a blouse. When making a garment, you accomplish reversed pieces when cutting the pattern on two layers of fabric placed with right sides together. This can be done when cutting templates as well.

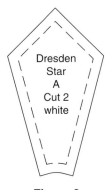

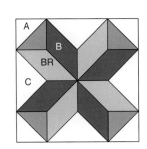

Figure 3
Mark each template with the pattern name and piece identification.

Figure 4
This pattern uses reversed pieces.

If cutting one layer of fabric at a time, first trace the template onto the backside of the fabric with the marked side down; turn the template over with the marked side up to make reverse pieces.

Hand-Piecing Basics. When hand-piecing it is easier to

begin with templates that do not include the ¼" seam allowance. Place the template on the wrong side of the fabric, lining up the marked grain line with lengthwise or crosswise fabric grain. If the piece does not have to be reversed, place with labeled side up. Trace around shape; move, leaving ½" between the shapes, and mark again.

When you have marked the appropriate number of pieces, cut out pieces, leaving ¼" beyond marked line all around each piece.

To join two units, place the patches with right sides together. Stick a pin in at the beginning of the seam through both fabric patches, matching the beginning points (Figure 5); for hand-piecing, the seam begins on the traced line, not at the edge of the fabric (see Figure 6).

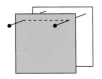

Figure 5
Stick a pin through fabrics to match the beginning of the seam.

Figure 6
Begin hand-piecing at seam, not at the edge of the fabric. Continue stitching along seam line.

Thread a sharp needle; knot one strand of the thread at the end. Remove the pin and insert the needle in the hole; make a short stitch and then a backstitch right over the first stitch. Continue making short stitches with several stitches on the needle at one time. As you stitch, check the back piece often to assure accurate stitching on the seam line. Take a stitch at the end of the seam; backstitch and knot at the same time as shown in Figure 7. Seams on hand-pieced fabric patches may be finger-pressed toward the darker fabric.

To sew units together, pin fabric patches together, matching seams. Sew as above except where seams meet; at these intersections, backstitch, go through seam to next piece and backstitch again to secure seam joint.

Not all pieced blocks can be stitched with straight seams or in rows. Some patterns require set-in pieces. To begin a set-in seam, pin one side of the square to the proper side of the star point with right sides together, matching corners. Start stitching at the seam line on the outside point; stitch on the marked seam line to the end of the seam line at the center referring to Figure 8.

General Instructions

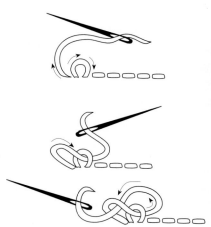

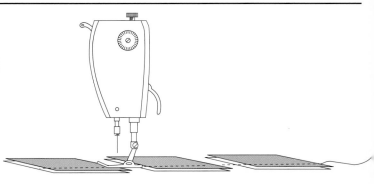

Figure 11
Units may be chain-pieced to save time.

Figure 7
Make a loop in backstitch to make a knot.

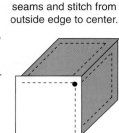

Figure 8
To set a square into a diamond point, match seams and stitch from outside edge to center.

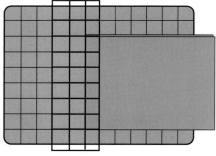

Figure 9
Continue stitching the adjacent side of the square to the next diamond shape in 1 seam from center to outside as shown.

Bring around the adjacent side and pin to the next star point, matching seams. Continue the stitching line from the adjacent seam through corners and to the outside edge of the square as shown in Figure 9.

Machine-Piecing. If making templates, include the ¼" seam allowance on the template for machine-piecing. Place template on the wrong side of the fabric as for hand-piecing except butt pieces against one another when tracing.

Set machine on 2.5 or 12–15 stitches per inch. Join pieces as for hand-piecing for set-in seams; but for other straight seams, begin and end sewing at the end of the fabric patch sewn as shown in Figure 10. No backstitching is necessary when machine-stitching.

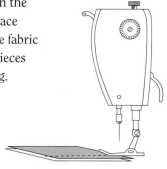

Figure 10
Begin machine-piecing at the end of the piece, not at the end of the seam.

Join units as for hand-piecing referring to the piecing diagrams where needed. Chain piecing (Figure 11—sewing several like units before sewing other units) saves time by eliminating beginning and ending stitches.

When joining machine-pieced units, match seams against each other with seam allowances pressed in opposite directions to

reduce bulk and make perfect matching of seams possible (Figure 12).

Quick-Cutting. Templates can be completely eliminated when using a rotary cutter with a plastic ruler and mat to cut fabric strips.

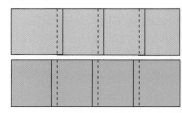

Figure 12
Sew machine-pieced units with seams pressed in opposite directions.

When rotary-cutting strips, straighten raw edges of fabric by folding fabric in fourths across the width as shown in Figure 13. Press down flat; place ruler on fabric square with edge of fabric and make one cut from the folded edge to the outside edge. If strips are not straightened, a wavy strip will result as shown in Figure 14.

Figure 13
Fold fabric and straighten as shown.

Figure 14
Wavy strips result if fabric is not straightened before cutting.

Always cut away from your body, holding the ruler firmly with the non-cutting hand. Keep fingers away from the edge of the ruler as it is easy for the rotary cutter to slip and jump over the edge of the ruler if cutting is not properly done.

If a square is required for the pattern, it can be subcut from a strip as shown in Figure 15.

Figure 15
If cutting squares, cut proper-width strip into same-width segments. Here, a 2" strip is cut into 2" segments to create 2" squares. These squares finish at 1 1/2" when sewn.

If you need right triangles with the straight grain on the short sides, you can use the same method, but you need to figure out how wide to cut the strip. Measure the finished size of one short side of the triangle. Add ⅞" to this size for seam allowance. Cut fabric strips this width; cut the strips into the same increment to create squares. Cut the squares on the diagonal to produce triangles. For example, if you need a triangle with a 2" finished height, cut the strips 2⅞" by the width of the fabric. Cut the strips into 2⅞" squares. Cut each square on the diagonal to produce the correct-size triangle with the grain on the short sides (Figure 16).

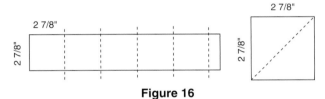

Figure 16
Cut 2" (finished size) triangles from 2 7/8" squares as shown.

Triangles sewn together to make squares are called half-square triangles or triangle/squares. When joined, the triangle/square unit has the straight of grain on all outside edges of the block.

Another method of making triangle/squares is shown in Figure 17. Layer two squares with right sides together; draw a diagonal line through the center. Stitch ¼" on both sides of the line. Cut apart on the drawn line to reveal two stitched triangle/squares.

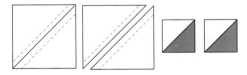

Figure 17
Mark a diagonal line on the square; stitch 1/4" on each side of the line. Cut on line to reveal stitched triangle/squares.

If you need triangles with the straight of grain on the diagonal, such as for fill-in triangles on the outside edges of a diagonal-set quilt, the procedure is a bit different.

To make these triangles, a square is cut on both diagonals; thus, the straight of grain is on the longest or diagonal side (Figure

18). To figure out the size to cut the square, add 1¼" to the needed finished size of the longest side of the triangle. For example, if you need a triangle with a 12" finished diagonal, cut a 13¼" square.

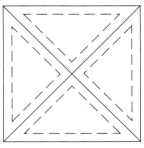

Figure 18
Add 1 1/4" to the finished size of the longest side of the triangle needed and cut on both diagonals to make a quarter-square triangle.

If templates are given, use their measurments to cut fabric strips to correspond with that measurement. The template may be used on the strip to cut pieces quickly. Strip cutting works best for squares, triangles, rectangles and diamonds. Odd-shaped templates are difficult to cut in multiple layers or using a rotary cutter.

Quick-Piecing Method. Lay pieces to be joined under the presser foot of the sewing machine right sides together. Sew an exact ¼" seam allowance to the end of the piece; place another unit right next to the first one and continue sewing, adding a piece after every stitched piece, until all of the pieces are used up (Figure 19).

Figure 19
Sew pieces together in a chain.

When sewing is finished, cut threads joining the pieces apart. Press seam toward the darker fabric.

Appliqué

Appliqué. Appliqué is the process of applying one piece of fabric on top of another for decorative or functional purposes.

Making Templates. Most appliqué designs given here are shown as full-size drawings for the completed designs. The drawings show dotted lines to indicate where one piece overlaps another. Other marks indicate placement of embroidery stitches for decorative purposes such as eyes, lips, flowers, etc.

For hand appliqué, trace each template onto the right side of the fabric with template right side up. Cut around shape, adding a ⅛"–¼" seam allowance.

Before the actual appliqué process begins, cut the background block. If you have a full-size drawing of the design, it might help you to draw on the background block to help with placement.

General Instructions

Transfer the design to a large piece of tracing paper. Place the paper on top of the design; use masking tape to hold in place. Trace design onto paper.

If you don't have a light box, tape the pattern on a window; center the background block on top and tape in place. Trace the design onto the background block with a water-erasable marker or light lead or chalk pencil. This drawing will mark exactly where the fabric pieces should be placed on the background block.

Hand Appliqué. Traditional hand appliqué uses a template made from the desired finished shape without seam allowance added.

After fabric is prepared, trace the desired shape onto the right side of the fabric with a water-erasable marker or light lead or chalk pencil. Leave at least ½" between design motifs when tracing to allow for the seam allowance when cutting out the shapes.

When the desired number of shapes needed has been drawn on the fabric pieces, cut out shapes leaving ⅛"–¼" all around drawn line for turning under.

Turn the shape's edges over on the drawn or stitched line. When turning in concave curves, clip to seams and baste the seam allowance over as shown in Figure 20.

Figure 20
Concave curves should be clipped before turning as shown.

During the actual appliqué process, you may be layering one shape on top of another. Where two fabrics overlap, the underneath piece does not have to be turned under or stitched down.

If possible, trim away the underneath fabric when the block is finished by carefully cutting away the background from underneath and then cutting away unnecessary layers to reduce bulk and avoid shadows from darker fabrics showing through on light fabrics.

For hand appliqué, position the fabric shapes on the background block and pin or baste them in place. Using a blind stitch or appliqué stitch, sew pieces in place with matching thread and small stitches. Start with background pieces first and work up to foreground pieces. Appliqué the pieces in place on the background in numerical order, if given, layering as necessary.

Machine Appliqué. There are several products available to help make the machine-appliqué process easier and faster.

Fusible transfer web is a commercial product similar to iron-on interfacings except it has two sticky sides. It is used to adhere appliqué shapes to the background with heat. Paper is adhered to one side of the web.

To use, reverse pattern and draw shapes onto the paper side of the web; cut, leaving a margin around each shape. Place on the wrong side of the chosen fabric; fuse in place referring to the manufacturer's instructions. Cut out shapes on the drawn line. Peel off the paper and fuse in place on the background fabric. Transfer any detail lines to the fabric shapes. This process adds a little bulk or stiffness to the appliquéd shape and makes hand-quilting through the layers difficult.

For successful machine appliqué a tear-off stabilizer is recommended. This product is placed under the background fabric while machine appliqué is being done. It is torn away when the work is finished. This kind of stabilizer keeps the background fabric from pulling during the machine-appliqué process.

During the actual machine-appliqué process, you will be layering one shape on top of another. Where two fabrics overlap, the underneath piece does not have to be turned under or stitched down.

Thread the top of the machine with thread to match the fabric patches or with threads that coordinate or contrast with fabrics. Rayon thread is a good choice when a sheen is desired on the finished appliqué stitches. Do not use rayon thread in the bobbin; use all-purpose thread.

When all machine work is complete, remove stabilizer from the back referring to the manufacturer's instructions.

Putting It All Together

Finishing the Top
Settings. Most quilts are made by sewing individual blocks together in rows that, when joined, create a design. There are several other methods used to join blocks. Sometimes the setting choice is determined by the block's design. For example, a House block should be placed upright on a quilt, not sideways or upside down.

Plain blocks can be alternated with pieced or appliquéd blocks in a straight set. Making a quilt using plain blocks saves time; half the number of pieced or appliquéd blocks are needed to make the same-size quilt as shown in Figure 1.

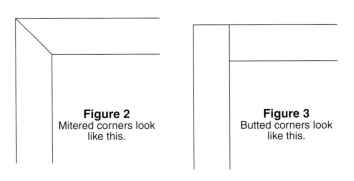

Figure 1
Alternate plain blocks with pieced blocks to save time.

Adding Borders. Borders are an integral part of the quilt and should complement the colors and designs used in the quilt center. Borders frame a quilt just like a mat and frame do a picture.

If fabric strips are added for borders, they may be mitered or butted at the corners as shown in Figures 2 and 3. To determine the size for butted border strips, measure across the center of the completed quilt top from one side raw edge to the other side raw edge. This measurement will include a ¼" seam allowance.

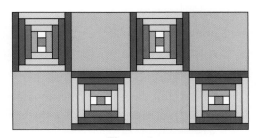

Figure 2
Mitered corners look like this.

Figure 3
Butted corners look like this.

Cut two border strips that length by the chosen width of the border. Sew these strips to the top and bottom of the pieced center referring to Figure 4. Press the seam allowance toward the border strips.

Measure across the completed quilt top at the center, from top raw edge to bottom raw edge, including the two border strips already added. Cut two border strips that length by the chosen width of the border. Sew a strip to each of the two remaining sides as shown in Figure 4. Press the seams toward the border strips.

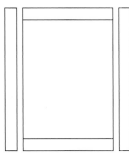

Figure 4
Sew border strips to opposite sides; sew remaining 2 strips to remaining sides to make butted corners.

To make mitered corners, measure the quilt as before. To this add twice the width of the border and ½" for seam allowances to determine the length of the strips. Repeat for opposite sides. Sew on each strip, stopping stitching ¼" from corner, leaving the remainder of the strip dangling.

Press corners at a 45-degree angle to form a crease. Stitch from the inside quilt corner to the outside on the creased line. Trim excess away after stitching and press mitered seams open (Figures 5–7).

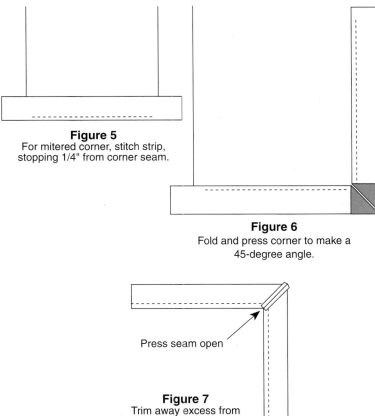

Figure 5
For mitered corner, stitch strip, stopping 1/4" from corner seam.

Figure 6
Fold and press corner to make a 45-degree angle.

Press seam open

Figure 7
Trim away excess from underneath when stitching is complete. Press seams open.

Carefully press the entire piece, including the pieced center. Avoid pulling and stretching while pressing, which would distort shapes.

General Instructions

Getting Ready to Quilt

Choosing a Quilting Design. If you choose to hand- or machine-quilt your finished top, you will need to select a design for quilting.

There are several types of quilting designs, some of which may not have to be marked. The easiest of the unmarked designs is in-the-ditch quilting. Here the quilting stitches are placed in the valley created by the seams joining two pieces together or next to the edge of an appliqué design. There is no need to mark a top for in-the-ditch quilting. Machine quilters choose this option because the stitches are not as obvious on the finished quilt. (Figure 8).

Outline-quilting ¼" or more away from seams or appliqué shapes is another no-mark alternative (Figure 9) that prevents having to sew through the layers made by seams, thus making stitching easier.

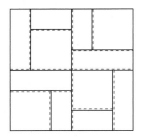
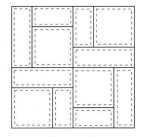

Figure 8
In-the-ditch quilting is done in the seam that joins 2 pieces.

Figure 9
Outline-quilting 1/4" away from seam is a popular choice for quilting.

If you are not comfortable eyeballing the ¼" (or other distance), masking tape is available in different widths and is helpful to place on straight-edge designs to mark the quilting line. If using masking tape, place the tape right up against the seam and quilt close to the other edge.

Meander or free-motion quilting by machine fills in open spaces and doesn't require marking. It is fun and easy to stitch as shown in Figure 10.

Marking the Top for Quilting. If you choose a fancy or allover design for quilting, you will need to transfer the design to your quilt top before layering with the backing and batting. You may

Figure 10
Machine meander quilting fills in large spaces.

use a sharp medium-lead or silver pencil on light background fabrics. Test the pencil marks to guarantee that they will wash out of your quilt top when quilting is complete; or be sure your quilting stitches cover the pencil marks. Mechanical pencils with very fine points may be used successfully to mark quilts.

Manufactured quilt-design templates are available in many designs and sizes and are cut out of a durable plastic template material that is easy to use.

To make a permanent quilt-design template, choose a template material on which to transfer the design. See-through plastic is the best as it will let you place the design while allowing you to see where it is in relation to your quilt design without moving it. Place the design on the quilt top where you want it and trace around it with your marking tool. Pick up the quilting template and place again; repeat marking.

No matter what marking method you use, remember—the marked lines should never show on the finished quilt. When the top is marked, it is ready for layering.

Preparing the Quilt Backing. The quilt backing is a very important feature of your quilt. The materials listed for each quilt in this book includes the size requirements for the backing, not the yardage needed. Exceptions to this are when the backing fabric is also used on the quilt top and yardage is given for that fabric.

A backing is generally cut at least 4" larger than the quilt top or 2" larger on all sides. For a 64" x 78" finished quilt, the backing would need to be at least 68" x 82".

To avoid having the seam across the center of the quilt backing, cut or tear one of the right-length pieces in half and sew half to each side of the second piece as shown in Figure 11.

Quilts that need a backing more than 88" wide may be pieced in horizontal pieces as shown in Figure 12.

Layering the Quilt Sandwich. Layering the quilt top with the batting and backing is time-consuming. Open the batting several days before you need it and place over a bed or flat on the floor to help flatten the creases caused from its being folded up in the bag for so long.

Iron the backing piece, folding in half both vertically and horizontally and pressing to mark centers.

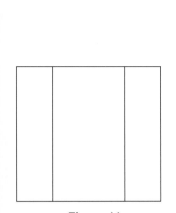

Figure 11
Center 1 backing piece
with a piece on each side.

Figure 12
Horizontal seams may be
used on backing pieces.

If you will not be quilting on a frame, place the backing right side down on a clean floor or table. Start in the center and push any wrinkles or bunches flat. Use masking tape to tape the edges to the floor or large clips to hold the backing to the edges of the table. The backing should be taut.

Place the batting on top of the backing, matching centers using fold lines as guides; flatten out any wrinkles. Trim the batting to the same size as the backing.

Fold the quilt top in half lengthwise and place on top of the batting, wrong side against the batting, matching centers. Unfold quilt and, working from the center to the outside edges, smooth out any wrinkles or lumps.

To hold the quilt layers together for quilting, baste by hand or use safety pins. If basting by hand, thread a long thin needle with a long piece of unknotted white or off-white thread. Starting in the center and leaving a long tail, make 4"–6" stitches toward the outside edge of the quilt top, smoothing as you baste. Start at the center again and work toward the outside as shown in Figure 13.

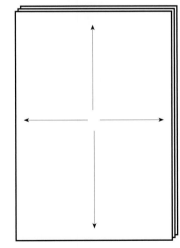

Figure 13
Baste from the center to the outside edges.

If quilting by machine, you may prefer to use safety pins for holding your fabric sandwich together. Start in the center of the quilt and pin to the outside, leaving pins open until all are placed. When you are satisfied that all layers are smooth, close the pins.

Quilting

Hand Quilting. Hand quilting is the process of placing stitches through the quilt top, batting and backing to hold them together. While it is a functional process, it also adds beauty and loft to the finished quilt.

To begin, thread a sharp between needle with an 18" piece of quilting thread. Tie a small knot in the end of the thread. Position the needle about ½" to 1" away from the starting point on quilt top. Sink the needle through the top into the batting layer but not through the backing. Pull the needle up at the starting point of the quilting design. Pull the needle and thread until the knot sinks through the top into the batting (Figure 14).

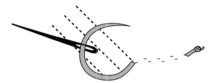

Figure 14
Start the needle through the top layer of fabric 1/2"–1"
away from quilting line with knot on top of fabric.

Some stitchers like to take a backstitch here at the beginning while others prefer to begin the first stitch here. Take small, even running stitches along the marked quilting line (Figure 15). Keep one hand positioned underneath to feel the needle go all the way through to the backing.

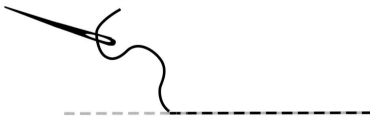

Figure 15
Make small, even running stitches on marked quilting line.

When you have nearly run out of thread, wind the thread around the needle several times to make a small knot and pull it close to the fabric. Insert the needle into the fabric on the quilting line and come out with the needle ½" to 1" away,

General Instructions

pulling the knot into the fabric layers the same as when you started. Pull and cut thread close to fabric. The end should disappear inside after cutting. Some quilters prefer to take a backstitch with a loop through it for a knot to end.

Machine Quilting. Successful machine quilting requires practice and a good relationship with your sewing machine.

Prepare the quilt for machine quilting in the same way as for hand quilting. Use safety pins to hold the layers together instead of basting with thread.

Presser-foot quilting is best used for straight-line quilting because the presser bar lever does not need to be continually lifted.

Set the machine on a longer stitch length (3.0 or 8–10 stitches to the inch). Too tight a stitch causes puckering and fabric tucks, either on the quilt top or backing. An even-feed or walking foot helps to eliminate the tucks and puckering by feeding the upper and lower layers through the machine evenly. Before you begin, loosen the amount of pressure on the presser foot.

Special machine-quilting needles work best to penetrate the three layers in your quilt.

Decide on a design. Quilting in the ditch is not quite as visible, but if you quilt with the feed dogs engaged, it means turning the quilt frequently. It is not easy to fit a rolled-up quilt through the small opening on the sewing machine head.

Meander quilting is the easiest way to machine-quilt—and it is fun. Meander quilting is done using an appliqué or darning foot with the feed dogs dropped. It is sort of like scribbling. Simply move the quilt top around under the foot and make stitches in a random pattern to fill the space. The same method may be used to outline a quilt design. The trick is the same as in hand quilting; you are striving for stitches of uniform size. Your hands are in complete control of the design.

If machine quilting is of interest to you, there are several very good books available at quilt shops that will help you become a successful machine quilter.

Finishing the Edges

After your quilt is tied or quilted, the edges need to be finished. Decide how you want the edges of your quilt finished before layering the backing and batting with the quilt top.

Without Binding—Self-Finish. There is one way to eliminate adding an edge finish. This is done before quilting. Place the batting on a flat surface. Place the pieced top right side up on the batting. Place the backing right sides together with the pieced top. Pin and/or baste the layers together to hold flat referring to Layering the Quilt Sandwich.

Begin stitching in the center of one side using a ¼" seam allowance, reversing at the beginning and end of the seam. Continue stitching all around and back to the beginning side. Leave a 12" or larger opening. Clip corners to reduce excess. Turn right side out through the opening. Slipstitch the opening closed by hand. The quilt may now be quilted by hand or machine.

The disadvantage to this method is that once the edges are sewn in, any creases or wrinkles that might form during the quilting process cannot be flattened out. Tying is the preferred method for finishing a quilt constructed using this method.

Bringing the backing fabric to the front is another way to finish the quilt's edge without binding. To accomplish this, complete the quilt as for hand or machine quilting. Trim the batting only even with the front. Trim the backing 1" larger than the completed top all around.

Turn the backing edge in ½" and then turn over to the front along edge of batting. The folded edge may be machine-stitched close to the edge through all layers, or blind-stitched in place to finish.

The front may be turned to the back. If using this method, a wider front border is needed. The backing and batting are trimmed 1" smaller than the top and the top edge is turned under ½" and then turned to the back and stitched in place.

One more method of self-finish may be used. The top and backing may be stitched together by hand at the edge. To accomplish this, all quilting must be stopped ½" from the quilt-top edge. The top and backing of the quilt are trimmed even and the batting is trimmed to ¼"–½" smaller. The edges of the top and backing are turned in ¼"–½" and blind-stitched together at the very edge.

These methods do not require the use of extra fabric and save time in preparation of binding strips; they are not as durable as an added binding.

Binding. The technique of adding extra fabric at the edges of the quilt is called binding. The binding encloses the edges and adds an extra layer of fabric for durability.

To prepare the quilt for the addition of the binding, trim the batting and backing layers flush with the top of the quilt using a rotary cutter and ruler or shears. Using a walking-foot attachment (sometimes called an even-feed foot attachment), machine-baste the three layers together all around approximately ⅛" from the cut edge.

The materials listed for each quilt in this book often includes a number of yards of self-made or purchased binding. Bias binding may be purchased in packages and in many colors. The advantage to self-made binding is that you can use fabrics from your quilt to coordinate colors. Double-fold, straight-grain binding and double-fold, bias-grain binding are two of the most commonly used types of binding.

Double-fold, straight-grain binding is used on smaller projects with right-angle corners. Double-fold, bias-grain binding is best suited for bed-size quilts or quilts with rounded corners.

To make double-fold, straight-grain binding, cut 2¼"-wide strips of fabric across the width or down the length of the fabric totaling the perimeter of the quilt plus 10". The strips are joined as shown in Figure 16 and pressed in half wrong sides together along the length using an iron on a cotton setting with no steam.

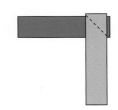

Figure 16
Join binding strips in a diagonal seam to eliminate bulk as shown.

Lining up the raw edges, place the binding on the top of the quilt and begin sewing (again using the walking foot) approximately 6" from the beginning of the binding strip. Stop sewing ¼" from the first corner, leave the needle in the quilt, turn and sew diagonally to the corner as shown in Figure 17.

Fold the binding at a 45-degree angle up and away from the quilt as shown in Figure 18 and back down flush with the raw edges. Starting at the top raw edge of the quilt, begin sewing the next side as shown in Figure 19. Repeat at the next three corners.

As you approach the beginning of the binding strip, stop stitching and overlap the binding ½" from the edge; trim. Join the two ends with a ¼" seam allowance and press the seam open.

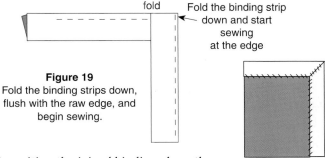

Sew diagonally off the corner of the quilt

binding strip

quilt

Figure 17
Sew to within 1/4" of corner; leave needle in quilt, turn and stitch diagonally off the corner of the quilt.

Fold the binding strip up at right angles

quilt

Figure 18
Fold binding at a 45-degree angle up and away from quilt as shown.

fold

Fold the binding strip down and start sewing at the edge

Figure 19
Fold the binding strips down, flush with the raw edge, and begin sewing.

Figure 20
Miter and stitch the corners as shown.

Reposition the joined binding along the edge of the quilt and resume stitching to the beginning.

To finish, bring the folded edge of the binding over the raw edges and blind-stitch the binding in place over the machine-stitching line on the backside. Hand-miter the corners on the back as shown in Figure 20.

If you are making a quilt to be used on a bed, you may want to use double-fold, bias-grain bindings because the many threads that cross each other along the fold at the edge of the quilt make it a more durable binding.

Cut 2¼"-wide bias strips from a large square of fabric. Join the strips as illustrated in Figure 16 and press the seams open. Fold the beginning end of the bias strip ¼" from the raw edge and press. Fold the joined strips in half along the long side, wrong sides together, and press with no steam (Figure 21).

Follow the same procedures as previously described for preparing the quilt top and sewing the binding to the quilt top. Treat the corners just as you treated them with straight-grain binding.

General Instructions

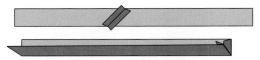

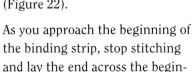

Figure 21
Fold and press strip in half.

Since you are using bias-grain binding, you do have the option to just eliminate the corners if this option doesn't interfere with the patchwork in the quilt. Round the corners off by placing one of your dinner plates at the corner and rotary-cutting the gentle curve (Figure 22).

As you approach the beginning of the binding strip, stop stitching and lay the end across the beginning so it will slip inside the fold. Cut the end at a 45-degree angle so the raw edges are contained inside the beginning of the strip (Figure 23). Resume stitching to the beginning. Bring the fold to the back of the quilt and hand-stitch as previously described.

Figure 22
Round corners to eliminate square-corner finishes.

Figure 23
End the binding strips as shown.

Overlapped corners are not quite as easy as rounded ones, but a bit easier than mitering. To make overlapped corners, sew binding strips to opposite sides of the quilt top. Stitch edges down to finish. Trim ends even.

Sew a strip to each remaining side, leaving 1½"–2" excess at each end. Turn quilt over and fold binding down even with previous finished edge as shown in Figure 24.

Fold binding in toward quilt and stitch down as before, enclosing the previous bound edge in the seam as shown in Figure 25. It may be necessary to trim the folded-down section to reduce bulk.

Figure 24
Fold end of binding even with previous page.

Figure 25
An overlapped corner is not quite as neat as a mitered corner.

Final Touches

If your quilt will be hung on the wall, a hanging sleeve is required. Other options include purchased plastic rings or fabric tabs. The best choice is a fabric sleeve, which will evenly distribute the weight of the quilt across the top edge, rather than at selected spots where tabs or rings are stitched, keep the quilt hanging straight and not damage the batting.

To make a sleeve, measure across the top of the finished quilt. Cut an 8"-wide piece of muslin equal to that length—you may need to seam several muslin strips together to make the required length.

Fold in ¼" on each end of the muslin strip and press. Fold again and stitch to hold. Fold the muslin strip lengthwise with right sides together. Sew along the long side to make a tube. Turn the tube right side out; press with seam at bottom or centered on the back.

Hand-stitch the tube along the top of the quilt and the bottom of the tube to the quilt back making sure the quilt lies flat. Stitches should not go through to the front of the quilt and don't need to be too close together as shown in Figure 26.

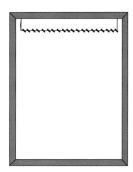

Figure 26
Sew a sleeve to the top back of the quilt.

Slip a wooden dowel or long curtain rod through the sleeve to hang.

When the quilt is finally complete, it should be signed and dated. Use a permanent pen on the back of the quilt. Other methods include cross-stitching your name and date on the front or back or making a permanent label which may be stitched to the back.